What some are saying about this book...

By describing the relational landscape in terms of moving from emotional adolescence to emotional adulthood, Larry Ellis paints a helpful picture of healthy differentiation that is tangible and practicable—and that points the way to human flourishing in our relationships. As a pastor, I value Ellis' insights into pursuing individuation and the importance of establishing healthy boundaries. Concurrently, I have been made more aware to when enmeshment or disconnection threatens healthy functioning—in my own relating and helping others in theirs. In sharing these insights with others, Ellis has challenged (and encouraged!) us all to pursue a God-honoring and life-giving relational future.

Fr. Chris Ditzenberger, Rector
St. Gabriel the Archangel Episcopal Church
Cherry Hills Village, CO

"The fall" of humanity led not only to the breakdown of relationship between humans and God but also to the breakdown in our relationships with each other. Dr. Ellis shows us how to understand, repair and reestablish those relationships. His book, Great Connections: Loving with Limits, *leads us on a journey to achieve healthy relationships with fascinating examples of psychological behaviors from the Bible. Dr. Ellis further provides us with diverse philosophies of counseling options for those seeking further insight into relationships.*

Richard B. Cole, Attorney at Law

This is a significant book on an important subject often overlooked by American Christianity. Larry Ellis does an excellent job of uncovering and highlighting valuable research in interpersonal relationships to the benefit of Christians in all walks of life. The foundation of ministry is relationships, and this book is an excellent resource for Christian leaders and lay people looking to grow in their relationships with others and with God.

Chris Hirschy, Pastor
Salem Magley Church
Decatur, IN

GREAT CONNECTIONS

Loving with Limits

Also written by Larry D. Ellis

Forgiveness: Unleashing a Transformational Process
www.theforgivenessbook.com

Secrets for a Successful Small Business: What the University Will Not Teach You
www.thesmallbusinessbook.com

Radical Worship: What Sunday Morning Can Never Give You
www.theradicalworshipbook.com

GREAT CONNECTIONS

Loving with Limits

Larry D. Ellis, DWS

Adoration Publishing Company
Denver, Colorado USA

Adoration Publishing Company
3767 South Jasmine Street
Denver CO 80237 USA
E-mail: info@adorationpublishing.com
www.adorationpublishing.com
www.theradicalworshipbook.com
www.theradicalworshipbook.com

Great Connections: Loving with Limits

Identifiers: ISBN 13, 978-0-9822464-8-1; 10, 0-9822464-8-X (softcover print)
                   13, 978-0-9822464-9-8; 10, 0-9822464-9-8 (digital)
           LCCN 2018901902

© Copyright 2018 by Larry D. Ellis

All rights reserved. No part of this book may be reproduced in any form without written permission from Adoration Publishing Company.

All Scripture quotations, unless otherwise indicated, are from the ESV® Bible (The Holy Bible, English Standard Version®), copyright © 2001 by Crossway, a publishing ministry of Good News Publishers. Used by permission. All rights reserved.

Book layout: Christian Diffenderfer
Graphics copyright © by A. and I. Kruk

Suggested Cataloging within the Library of Congress System

Ellis, Larry D. 1947-
Religion, Ethics, Conduct of life, relationships

Suggested Library of Congress Call Number: BJ1581.2 E45 2018

Suggested Dewey Decimal Cataloging: 248.4 Ellis

1.0.0

When we feel lonely we keep looking for a person or persons who can take our loneliness away. Our lonely hearts cry out, "Please hold me, touch me, speak to me, pay attention to me." But soon we discover that the person we expect to take our loneliness away cannot give us what we ask for. Often that person feels oppressed by our demands and runs away, leaving us in despair. As long as we approach another person from our loneliness, no mature human relationship can develop. Clinging to one another in loneliness is suffocating and eventually becomes destructive. For love to be possible we need the courage to create space between us and to trust that this space allows us to dance together.

                                        Henri Nouwen from *Creating a Space to Dance Together*

Contents

Glossary xi

Abbreviations for the Books of the Bible xiii

Foreword xv

Preface xvii

Introduction 1

1—Keeping a Positive Balance 7
    Characters in Play
    Jonathan Tries Hard to Keep Things in Balance
        Jonathan Has Not Established Limits on Expectations
    Dave Is Challenging to Everyone
        Dave's Reign Came to an End
    Rebecka Is Cut Off
        A Widow Forfeited Her Most Valued Relationships
    There is Hope for Change

2—The Destruction from Enmeshment 17
    Honoring Boundaries
    The Dangers of Enmeshment
    Emotions are Important Cues
    Enmeshed Behavior
    Enmeshed with God
    Counterfeit Unity
    Resistance Is Not Futile

3—The Debilitation of Disconnection 35
    The Nature of Disconnection
    The Action of Disconnection
    The Restoration from Disconnection
    Distinctions between Disconnection and Differentiations

4—The Surprises about Differentiation 41
    Differentiation Is Being Balanced
    God Is Differentiated from All Else
    God Divides
    The Differentiation of Humanity
    The Empowerment of Differentiation

5—God's Design for Humanity 53
    Made in the Image of God
    God Desires Unity
    God's Connected Design Elements

6—Boundaries Are Biblical 59
    Jesus Set Boundaries
    The Man with Two Lost Sons
    Nathan Courageously Confronts King David
    Other Prominent People with Strong Boundaries
        Moses
        Job
        Daniel
        Shadrach, Meshach, and Abednego
        Additional People with Strong Boundaries
    Living with Healthy Boundaries
    Insights from Scripture

7—The Distortion of Authority 79
    The Foundation of Authority
    Hearing God
    Authority over Other Persons' Lives

Authority over Our Children
False Authority of Enmeshment with God
Closing Thoughts on Authority

8—Moving into Liberation 107
Enmeshment Is against God's Design
Emancipation from Enmeshment
Liberation from Disconnection
Balance Individuality and Togetherness
Separate, Equal, and Open
Embracing Differentiation Is Challenging
Concluding Thoughts about Healthy Relationships

Appendix—Approaches to Counseling and Scripture. 121
Diverse Claims of Authenticity
Secular Counseling
Biblical Counseling
Holistic Counseling
The Wisdom of Counsel

Bibliography. 137

Index of Topics. 143

Scripture Index 145

Glossary

boundary. The physical, spiritual, and emotional limits we establish to protect ourselves against being violated or manipulated by others.

counterfeit. Something that is an imitation and is usually passed off deceptively as genuine.

differentiation. The process of living out of a proper balance between independence from others and togetherness with others, whereby the person is able to make their own choices about their life, not being controlled by other people's expectations and being willing to hear and understand points of view with which they do not agree. This is an essential element in identity formation and a precursor to intimacy.

disconnection. The intentional severing of a relationship, deciding no longer to be open to the roles of initiation or response that could possibly lead someone to strong friendship and intimacy.

enmeshment. The state of being emotionally or spiritually entangled with someone or something which makes independent thinking and autonomous decision-making difficult.

false identity. The image that someone believes to be true about oneself that stands in contrast to how that person really is.

fused. See enmeshment.

individuation. The process of discovering and learning to live out of one's authentic self, rather than promoting a false image of how that person would like to be perceived. It is the process where one develops a sense of unique distinction of themselves from other people. It involves separation and differentiation and allows for true intimacy.

Abbreviations for the Books of the Bible

Gen	Genesis	Hab	Habakkuk
Exod	Exodus	Zeph	Zephaniah
Lev	Leviticus	Hag	Haggai
Num	Numbers	Zech	Zechariah
Deut	Deuteronomy	Mal	Malachi
Josh	Joshua	Matt	Matthew
Judg	Judges	Mark	Mark
Ruth	Ruth	Luke	Luke
1, 2 Sam	1, 2 Samuel	John	John
1, 2 Kgs	1, 2 Kings	Acts	Acts
1, 2 Chr	1, 2 Chronicles	Rom	Romans
Ezra	Ezra	1, 2 Cor	1, 2 Corinthians
Neh	Nehemiah	Gal	Galatians
Esth	Esther	Eph	Ephesians
Job	Job	Phil	Philippians
Ps	Psalm(s)	Col	Colossians
Prov	Proverbs	1, 2 Thess	1, 2 Thessalonians
Eccl	Ecclesiastes	1, 2 Tim	1, 2 Timothy
Song	Song of Solomon	Titus	Titus
Isa	Isaiah	Phlm	Philemon
Jer	Jeremiah	Heb	Hebrews
Lam	Lamentations	Jas	James
Ezek	Ezekiel	1, 2 Pet	1, 2 Peter
Dan	Daniel	1, 2, 3 John	1, 2, 3 John
Hos	Hosea	Jude	Jude
Joel	Joel	Rev	Revelation
Amos	Amos		
Obad	Obadiah		
Jonah	Jonah		
Mic	Micah		
Nah	Nahum		

Foreword

When I first read Larry Ellis's manuscript, I thought, "everyone would benefit from practicing the suggestions he makes in his new book Great Connections." The terms might be unfamiliar to some, but the concepts are ones which I wish I had known early in my marriage. My wife and I had no ideas about how to set "boundaries" back in the sixties. Individuation, becoming our own person, was difficult, because neither of us really knew who we were as individuals. Of course, knowing ourselves beyond the roles of wife, husband, son, daughter, student, or employee, involve a growth process. Maturity and wisdom come with time and effort.

Larry goes into detail about those very topics—enmeshment, a system that keeps us from separating ourselves from others, boundaries, which has become a more familiar concept over the last twenty years, and individuation, being a person separate from those around us. Once we learn how to avoid being enmeshed, how to set boundaries, and how to become and be who we really are, we are able to have healthy relationships. In addition, learning the skill of being assertive (as opposed to being passive or aggressive), i.e. getting our needs met without disregarding the needs of others is indispensable.

Unfortunately, failing relationships are more the norm than the exception, as a good marriage is difficult to maintain. A good friend of mine often suggests that "marriage is a growing machine." Iron does sharpen iron, but only if we are willing to deal with the friction.

- Do you often wonder why some relationships thrive and last for a lifetime while others fail and fall apart?
- Do you often feel lonely, left out, rejected, or even abandoned?
- Do you have parts within you that are reasonably mature and successful, but then become aware that there are

other parts that are insecure, fearful, or hurt, which can literally sabotage your overall maturity and success?

Larry has done a masterful job of answering these questions and explaining the maturation process. He shows how interacting with others (parents, siblings, friends, and peers at work and school) can give us opportunities every day to handle situations with maturity.

I am excited to pass this book on to friends and clients. Practicing the loving concepts can make us more aware, empathetic, and sensitive to others, guaranteeing improvement in our relationships.

Jerry Donaldson,
Marriage and Family Counselor
former adjunct faculty at Denver Seminary

Preface

I was not an assertive person in my earlier days. I knew what I wanted, needed, and believed, but I certainly would not try to impose any of these perspectives upon my friends. I did not often risk much personal disclosure, because I wanted to avoid any form of rejection. As I advanced in the business world, I felt it was necessary to be more outgoing. That is how I saw effective leaders behave. I had observed some of my more aggressive co-workers and found them to be rather obnoxious. I did not want to be like that, but I forced myself to operate well outside my comfort zone when it came to managing projects at work. I presented a super-confident persona to those around me, but even when I stood firm against some who would disagree with me, the entire process drained me of a great deal of energy. That assertiveness did not spill over into my personal life.

The only meaning I knew for the word boundary was related to geography. Differentiation was simply a mathematical process one used in calculus. Most of the other terms I describe in this book were completely unknown to me. One thing that impacted me greatly was when my wife, Jill, told me she would rather know what I feel and think, even if she disagreed with it, than be left in the dark and have to guess. It was with her that I started my long journey of leaving emotional adolescence and began moving into emotional adulthood. I had a wealth of unhealthy processes to re-work in order to move ahead. Our work of learning to have healthy connections with those around us will never be completed. Each one of us is forever a work in progress.

This book is a direct result of my own experiences in receiving counseling, working through conflicts and frustration, and extensive research on some of the relational issues that have plagued me and many other Christians. No one writes a book without being influenced by many circumstances and people. A special thanks goes to my editor, Christine Ellis Kosoff. Her work on this project was invaluable. I would also like to thank those friends who have read through this manuscript and helped me expand my thinking process, research, and understanding. They are counselors, pastors, and profoundly competent professionals in the work force. You know who you are, and I thank you. As you read through this book, I hope that you will develop a deeper understanding about how to establish and maintain great friendships.

Larry D. Ellis

Introduction

This book addresses the demanding topic of establishing and continuing healthy relationships. We all long for vibrant relationships. Even so, our best efforts sometimes fall short of the successful connection and intimacy we desire. It is often easy for us to see opportunities for growth in other people's lives, but the greater challenge is to accurately assess our own success in relationships. We eventually learn that the only person over which we have control is ourselves, and even managing our own self can be difficult at times. We all need to learn how to better take responsibility for our own spiritual, emotional, and psychological health.

A good starting point will be to become familiar with the vocabulary words and their meanings that I have put forth in the glossary. These definitions explain how I have used these words in this book and are commonly accepted within much of the professional counseling community. Some of this vocabulary might be unfamiliar to people who have not studied the social sciences. A clear understanding of these words will be important in order to integrate much of the explanations presented here with one's personal experiences. We will examine a number of case studies of people with significant dysfunction. Some of these are fictional characters presented in short stories, although the dysfunctions are all taken from real life. Others will be case studies of biblical characters that represent emotional problems as well as some biblical characters who are particularly healthy. We will examine some of the recorded words of Jesus along with some of his direct actions concerning emotional and physical boundaries he established.

This book approaches healthy personal relationships from a Christian worldview. There are some theological underpinnings about God's creation of the earth and his design for humankind that shed light on how we can live harmoniously together. Christian theologians use the term "the fall" of humanity to describe the breakdown of relationships between humans and God. This breakdown occurred the moment Adam and Eve ate the forbidden fruit, an act of disobedience to God followed by blaming others for their own choices and actions.[1] In the same manner, our relationships also broke down as a result of our disobedience to God. Fortunately, God mercifully gave hope for our future redemption and reconciliation, but not without the consequence of brokenness we bring into creation by our disobedience. This is where our dysfunctions began. We will focus on two common dysfunctions, which appear as opposite extremes; one is being overly dependent with someone, and the other is being overly disconnected. I will discuss both of these extremes.

Finally, we will move into important areas that can bring liberation for those who feel trapped in unfulfilled relationships because of these dysfunctions. Throughout the book you will find a number of Scripture references and citations of other relevant material. I encourage you to examine these reference texts to learn more about the foundation for what I have written. Scripture provides a great deal of insight about how to wisely manage our relationships with others. The Bible records that after God created humans in his image, the first words God spoke to them were, "Be fruitful and multiply and fill the earth and subdue it, and have dominion over the fish of the sea and over the birds of the heavens and over every living thing that moves on the earth" (Gen 1:28). This revelation has enormous consequences. We are created to have dominion, which means our job is to take responsibility for managing ourselves well, along with managing all God has created and entrusted into our care. God has commissioned humanity to physically reproduce, but the challenge of being fruitful means more than physical reproduction. It means we are to be beneficial, effective, and successful. Our mission is also to wisely care for all God has created. I suggest that one of the most challenging areas for us to master is managing our own part of our

---

1. For more detail see Gen 3.

relationships with others. Learning to take ownership of our feelings and actions has not become easier since the days of creation.

I suggest a corollary that follows is we are also to know and avoid doing what is not our job. When we take on responsibilities that are not ours, we can experience unintended consequences. For example, we can exhaust ourselves and even irritate others, because we usurp other people's responsibilities. They might resent our invasion into what they believe is their responsibility. Conversely, one of the possible side effects is other people sometimes cheerfully welcome our lightening their load at our expense, because they no longer feel responsible. Either way, we do a disservice to ourselves and to them, should we try to manage people and things that are not our responsibility. By failing to take responsibility for what is our job or taking responsibility for what is not our job, we hinder the development of healthy relationships.

The driving force for this book is my desire to help the reader discover the destructive impact of unhealthy relationships and learn to relate to others as an emotionally healthy person. I hope you will not simply read this book as additional information on psychological and biblical teachings. I encourage you to reflect upon your own relationships, the good ones as well as the strained ones. Assess what you can do to strengthen all those relationships. None of us have reached full perfection . The list of lifestyle issues that are also important include living a life of kindness, generosity, sacrifice for others, humility, faithfulness, and honesty. These qualities will always be important but fall beyond the primary scope of this book. For those readers who wish to do further research on the subject I set forth, there are a few additional resources listed in the bibliography as well as an abundant supply of character-building values discussed throughout the Bible.[2]

---

2. Some significant examples might include Jesus' Sermon on the Mount in Matt 5-7 and Paul's instruction to the Christians at Galatia about the fruit of the Holy Spirit in the believer's life, found in Gal 5:16-24.

While the psychological terms of enmeshment, disconnection, differentiation, individuation, and boundaries are not explicitly found within the Scriptures, the Bible does provide an ample supply of behavioral examples of each of these important concepts. In this book, I will point out and analyze a number of these behaviors from both the Old and New Testament records. While the events in many of these historic records and parables are well known, examination from this frame of reference will present important insights about relationships. I will address both the establishment of good boundaries for the individual and the importance of respecting boundaries set by other people.

A particular focus will be an understanding of enmeshment with God, in which some people believe they are so clear about God's understanding that they see no distinction between their own perspective and God's point of view. When this enmeshment is in play, such a person can ensure the outcome they believe is appropriate, because they believe they have heard God's explicit direction, even when the decision negatively impacts others and may violate the other's own perceptions. When someone operates in such a way, there is no room for discussion, since "God has spoken" to them. Dysfunctional behavior can often be couched in spiritual language which makes dialogue with others who have a different perception virtually impossible.

There can be times when we feel stuck in our process of self-awareness or in how to resolve a problem-ridden relationship. We must develop wisdom to know what to do and what not to do in our relationships. We have the benefit of family and good friends, the wisdom in Scripture, spiritual teachers, and sometimes the guidance of wise counselors and therapists to assist us with our learning. It might come as a surprise to learn that there are many types of counselors available in our marketplace. If you desire help, in the appendix, I have included a significant discussion of several divergent philosophies of counseling to assist you in seeking the type of counselor that might be most beneficial to you. Each of us must rise to the challenge of recognizing and wisely carrying out the process of establishing and maintaining healthy relationships. As we deepen our personal relationships with sharpened discernment and intentional behavior, we will enjoy the benefits of freedom in independent living as well as meaningful intimacy with those around us.

Chapter 1

Keeping a Positive Balance

Characters in Play

The following characters represent a composite of real emotional/relational issues illustrating the concepts I wish to develop. The characters embody a combination of dis-empowering emotional behaviors from which they could be liberated if they would accept constructive spiritual and emotional help. As you read through these stories, strive to identify some of the problems in the ways the characters relate to one another. The rest of this book will help reveal these destructive patterns we all encounter. A goal of this book is to provide some guidance for the reader to establish and maintain healthy relationships when these dysfunctions are discovered within one's self.

Jonathan Tries Hard to Keep Things in Balance

Jonathan is a thirty-eight-year-old college graduate, a husband, and a dad. He works hard in his home remodeling business helping to provide for his family. He gets up early each work day to get underway at his construction office. It is important to him to get an early start, because his work environment can become chaotic as the day progresses. This morning he received two email inquiries about possible new projects. He must respond to them right away, because he wants to continually secure contracts for new projects. Throughout the day, there are endless phone calls from clients, in-person meetings with clients, emergency calls from sub-contractors, and calls from vendors who are out of stock of materials that were to have been delivered to the job sites. Clients frequently show up late for their appointments. Often, this behavior results in delaying meetings he has scheduled. Upon checking his company web site, he learned it has stopped working. When he checked his business checking account on-line this morning, he saw one of the deposits he made from a customer two days ago was returned for insufficient funds. In addition to these stresses, several of his clients have complained to him about not getting their projects completed by the deadlines he had promised. Jonathan strives for organization in his work, but endless interruptions make his day feel like he never gets to finish anything on time. His work days frequently end with very few of his planned tasks being completed.

Stresses also fill Jonathan's personal life. His wife works at a challenging job dealing with the public all day long. Their days off are often out of sync, so he cannot spend as much time with her as he would like. At six p.m. on work days, he drops by the childcare center to pick up Jennifer, their four-year-old daughter. When they arrive home in the evening, they must go shopping, prepare meals, and pay attention to their two dogs. He and his wife spend some time playing with Jennifer, read a story to her, and pray with her as they tuck her into bed. They share housekeeping chores after Jennifer has gone to sleep. Because of his demanding schedule, he has also not been able to volunteer at Jennifer's child-care center on a regular basis, which the center requires for each family. The couple enjoys several pay-per-view sporting events each month with a few of their friends. To know current events in the world, he tries to keep up on the news by checking several phone news apps throughout the day.

Jonathan's dad passed away a few years ago, and his mom now lives in a nearby assisted living facility. She wants him to stop by as often as he can and bring Jennifer, but he cannot seem to get by more often than a once each week. His mom frequently expresses her loneliness and how her life is so hard since his dad passed away. She also complains that her meals served at the facility are not very appetizing. Jonathan now serves as her primary care person, and he pays all her bills and regularly manages her few financial transactions. For many years, she sacrificed to raise him. He is as loving toward her now in her times of need as she was for him earlier in life. From his early youth, both his family and his church instilled in him the virtue of helping others. He feels bad for her problems, but he does not see a better alternative.

Jonathan strives to keep everyone happy: his wife, their daughter, his mom, his friends, his customers, and his vendors. He and his wife do get out to enjoy a few concerts each year and an occasional movie, but he does not have time to do some of the things he used to enjoy so much: target practice at the gun range, playing his guitar, and reading. Even with all his chaos, he functions reasonably well with only five to six hours of sleep each night.

Jonathan always intends to do the right thing and act responsibly for all those who count on him. He struggles with both guilt and anger toward himself because of his many shortcomings. He can never seem to get everything done, no matter how hard he tries. At times, he gets angry with some of those people who demand so much from him. He often feels stressed and out of control. After all, a day has only twenty-four hours.

Jonathan Has Not Established Limits on Expectations

Jonathan's dysfunctions adversely impact his relationship with almost everyone, his family and his work relationships. He experiences conflict because he cannot do everything people expect of him. He believes not fulfilling the desires of all these people would mean he is a bad person. He functions as what some people call "a people pleaser." He regularly sacrifices himself and his responsibilities to avoid disappointing those around him. Yet, he overextends himself and in turn disappoints almost all the people he tries to help. Jonathan has difficulties establishing realistic expectations upon himself and mutually agreeable expectations that others place upon him. He must face the challenges of establishing healthy limits with others to protect himself, his business, and especially his family.

Dave Is Challenging to Everyone

Dave had been a much sought-after attorney. Dave attended church regularly, because relationships there helped him to make contact with potential clients. He had chosen a large Episcopal church in a wealthy neighborhood for just that reason. He has made several large contributions to the church. It is important to him that the church leaders know he is an influential person. At one of the events at church, he met a wonderful young lady, Carol. She could match his intellect, wit, and had similar interest in sports and politics. He invited her out to dinner, and they struck up a wonderful friendship that moved into marriage within eighteen months. Carol seemed a bit more religious than he, but he could live with that.

After five years with Jim, his law partner, the firm's business manager discovered several large deposits were missing from the escrow account. Jim had been embezzling money from the firm's trust account. The firm was sued by two separate clients on this matter, and the court ruled in favor of the clients. Fortunately, while Jim had been stealing the money, Dave knew nothing of his partner's fraudulent behavior. Jim is now in the state penitentiary for eight years, and the firm is financially depleted. His relationship with his law partner has ended. Dave must now face the challenges of rebuilding the law practice and trying to regain the confidence of his few remaining clients.

For Dave, religion was okay, but mostly it was a way to get ahead in the world and promote his law practice. He and his wife continued to attend church regularly. However, Carol's behavior seemed more congruent with Christian values than Dave's. Because of all his accumulating financial and professional stresses, Dave decided to make a move outside of his normal behavior. He asked for an appointment with the priest to seek some advice as to how to find some balance in his life. After all, the priest did not charge for counseling. The priest told him about God's love for him and how he could begin to respond to that love. At that meeting, Dave made a serious commitment to God to have a relationship with him through Jesus. His new-found commitment began an exciting transformative process.

Dave knew he needed to change many things in his life. He began to read the Bible with the same intensity and passion he had with everything else. To learn more about God and what it means to follow him, he scaled back his law practice dramatically to free up some of his time, and he enrolled in a nearby seminary to study theology. After all, he knew there he would learn whatever he needed to do to become a faithful Christ-follower. That decision to enroll in seminary brought great joy to both Dave and Carol, because they saw this move as a major positive shift in his life. After two years in seminary, Dave sensed that God had wanted him to become a pastor. All who knew him were surprised by such a dramatic move, but Dave was clearly a man committed to making a meaningful life for himself. Upon graduation with his masters of divinity, he accepted a position as an associate pastor in a medium-sized church and eventually closed his law practice. Carol was proud of him and happily made the necessary adjustments to the changes in their standard of living from the earlier days of the lucrative law practice. After all, Dave felt nothing was more important than doing God's work as a spiritual leader. They believed they were both faithful to what was important to God.

Dave's personality, warm charisma, and intellect proved very useful in his new career. He began teaching the Bible. The small group he had started grew to over one hundred persons regularly attending his classes. Of course, his senior minister thought his class was great and often praised him publicly before the congregation. His obvious success made him feel quite accomplished. Dave readily enjoyed playing an influential role in the spiritual lives of people. They often came to him for advice. As long as they took his advice,

Dave was satisfied, but if they did not follow his advice, Dave was quite frustrated. He felt he provided enlightened advice. He was not only a seminary graduate, but he also had considerable business acumen. He felt personally responsible for the decisions his Bible students made. As time passed, the knowledge of a church member not following his counsel seemed to adversely affect his ability to relate to them.

In time, a larger church approached him and asked him to apply for their open position of senior pastor. Naturally, Dave thought bigger was obviously better. A larger church could pay him an increased salary. There would be more opportunities for expanded ministries in a larger church with a larger budget and a paid staff for him to guide and oversee. Such a move would also eliminate the need to maneuver around his current senior minister, when Dave needed to implement his passionate agendas that were not embraced by his pastor. Dave believed he would do a great job with the leadership skills he had acquired while running his law firm. Upon being selected, he accepted his new prestigious position.

Dave's outgoing personality and organized management skills gripped the new church at the onset. He was thrilled to lead a great church that would grow to become even greater with him at the helm. Not long after his arrival Dave began to notice some things in the church he felt were not optimum. Dave wanted his own personal assistant. The church had only one secretary who assisted the entire staff. On his own, he began to seek out candidates and conduct interviews for this new position. He felt he did not have time to fill out expense reimbursement forms, which had long been the practice in order to receive reimbursement for church-related expenses. He instructed the treasurer simply to issue checks to him for the amounts he turned in weekly without providing the supporting documentation.

Because it was important to support the financial needs of the church, he asked the financial secretary to provide him with a spreadsheet with a list of members along with their total financial contributions for the past year. He knew it was important to build relationships with the large contributors to the church. This way, should a monetary need arise, he would know whom he should approach.

Dave's style of being overly aggressive and defensive, blaming behavior ultimately brought forth his demise. The board at the church met with him and confronted him about overstepping his authority. He did not believe he had done anything wrong. He saw the board, rather than his own behavior, as the problem. After all, the decisions he had made were made for the benefit of the ministry. Dave continued to move ahead with his own agendas. He became worn out, because it took so much energy to take care of all he had to do. About a year later, the church board asked for his resignation. He felt blindsided by their decision.

Dave's Reign Came to an End

While Dave had no problem knowing and communicating what he wanted and required from others, but he had great difficulty respecting reasonable boundaries of other people around him. He felt he was a special gift to the church and his thoughts and wisdom should be imposed on others, regardless of their desires. He did not allow others to maintain their independence and integrity—respecting their preferences and decisions. Because of his autocratic lifestyle, only the strongest of personalities could maintain ownership of their own boundaries around Dave. Living this way built impenetrable walls between himself and others. He was manipulative and often self-centered. He was not approachable. People would often avoid him to protect themselves from his dominating personality. Dave cannot have healthy relationships with others especially when they disagree with him. His dysfunction impacted almost every area of his life.

Rebecka Is Cut Off

Rebecka has been married for nine years to Richard, the man she has loved since high school. They have a seven year old daughter and a son who is five. Rebecka's dad had loved them unconditionally until his unexpected death three years ago. They were still a happy family—until Rebecka's mom entered into their relationship. Her mom was never willing to fully accept Richard. Even before they were married, her mom frequently shamed him for his unsophisticated manner. Richard was a factory worker who was reliable and provided a steady income for the family. Yet Rebecka's mom felt her daughter could have had a much better life if she had married a man who was in her socio-economic class. After all, Rebecka had been the prom queen for her senior class. She could easily have married any number of higher-class men. Her mom was relentless in trying to pressure Rebecka to live her life as her mom believed best. She did not approve of their home, furniture, cars, or the public school where their kids were doing so well. She even felt she knew better how the patio furniture should be arranged. When they invited her over for a family BBQ, Richard always needed instructions on how to cook the food and arrange the dishes on the picnic table.

Rebecka was happy to have her own home, a loving husband, and two kids who behaved themselves most of the time. Richard was always cordial toward Rebecka's mom, but after all these years of stress, he was struggling to cope with her unceasing criticism of him. Rebecka was frequently torn between supporting her husband and the choices they had made versus those that her mom would have preferred. Sometimes Rebecka simply gave in to her mom's requests when she could no longer tolerate the incessant conflicts. Other times she would stew inside as she neared her limit of her mom's attempt to control them.

On one Saturday afternoon, a truck pulled up in front of their home while Rebecka was out shopping. Only Richard and the kids were at home. The truck was delivering a surprise gift for the family from her mom—a new sofa and a dining table and chairs. The fabric on their present sofa had a color and texture her mom never liked. She had selected something she felt was much more suitable for them to enjoy. The delivery people had been instructed to remove their replaced furniture and drop it off at a nearby Goodwill store as a donation. Richard was outraged at the invasive presumptions of this woman who had plagued them for years. He refused the delivery and sent the driver away with an unambiguous message for Rebecka's mother. When Rebecka returned home and heard what had happened, she was pushed over her limit. Together, they decided they would no longer tolerate the stress of her relationship with them. They called a friend to come over and sit with the kids, and they drove to her mom's house. They informed her that from now on, she was not welcome at their home; she was not to send any gifts to them or the kids. For them, she no longer existed. They were thoroughly exhausted from trying to manage her unwelcome interventions.

Rebecka's mom was surprised and hurt by their actions. After all, she was just trying to do something loving for her daughter's family who constantly needed her guidance. Three years passed, and she had still not heard anything from Rebecka and Richard, even though she had mailed birthday cards with checks to each member of the family every year. None of the cards were sent back and none of the checks had ever been cashed.

A Widow Forfeited Her Most Valued Relationships

Rebecka's mom did not respect many of the choices her daughter's family had made. Rebecka and Richard had always struggled to remain polite and forgiving toward her mom, hoping some day she would stop her criticism of how they lived their lives. After stuffing their wounded feelings for years, they could not endure her mom's judgments any longer. Rebecka had experienced so much pain in her relationship with her mom she completely cut herself and her family off from her. This decision was painful for her mom to endure; for Rebecka, it seemed to remove a great deal of stress between Richard and her. The severing of their relationship with her mom brought no hope of reconciliation, only isolation from her mom for Rebecka and her family. As long as Rebecka was disconnected from her mom, their relationship would never become close, and her mom had little choice but simply to exist without contact with her daughter's family.

There is Hope for Change

Neither the level of education, income level, gender, nor the professional skill level one has achieved can sufficiently protect anyone from these relational distortions of enmeshment and disconnection. Our hearts must be changed through our discovery of what God designed us to become. In the next chapters I will introduce and explain many important psychological terms that might be unfamiliar. We will examine important concepts that will help address some of these dysfunctions. Rather than embrace the counterfeit solutions of either being overly emotionally tied to someone or cutting ourselves off from others, the wisest solution is to learn to become more spiritually and emotionally balanced. The balance is being able to connect with others while maintaining one's own identity. Chapter 4 presents many details about the importance and process of learning to live in balance. That lifestyle alone will not always ensure healthy relationships, but living this way will empower individuals to operate much more successfully especially amid conflicting situations.

Chapter 2

The Destruction from Enmeshment

Honoring Boundaries

Boundaries define us. Our boundaries are the physical, spiritual, and emotional limits we establish to protect ourselves against being violated or manipulated by others. Healthy boundaries empower us to distinguish who we are, what we believe, and what we feel from the thoughts, beliefs, and feelings other people have. "They define what is me and what is not me. A boundary shows me where I end and someone else begins, leading me to a sense of ownership."[1]

When we think of boundaries, consider the border of one country that adjoins the border of another country. The United States governs real estate by the laws of the United States. Mexico and Canada regulate their own countries by their respective laws. Nations can cooperate with each other as long as both countries respect and honor their mutual boundaries. Should one of the countries decide to violate the sovereign space of an adjacent country, there will be serious, adverse consequences. Our relationships with other people operate the same way.

A picture of two inflated balloons presents a helpful image. One balloon can be larger than the other, or they can be the same size. One can be red and the other blue. Neither the balloons nor the colors combine when the balloons touch; each remains distinct. The

---

1. Henry Cloud and John Townsend, *Boundaries: When to Say Yes, How to Say No, How to Take Control of Your Life* (Grand Rapids, MI: Zondervan, 1992), 31.

larger the area of contact, the more they have in common. When they touch, there is no problem unless one pushes too hard against the other. When that condition happens, one of them will likely pop and no longer be able to enjoy its life as a colorful balloon. It will have been violated; it will have lost its identity.

Every football player, coach, and fan knows the explicit physical boundaries of the playing field. They also know the mental boundaries in play when they know the rules of the game. When a player or coach attempts to operate outside any of these boundaries, the referee will impose a penalty upon them. In our relationships with others, there are no neutral referees requiring all players to operate within the rules. We must become our own advocate for the relational boundaries we establish and define the limits of how others must relate to us. We must not live trying to please everyone and meet all of their unlimited expectations of us. Neither should we expect anyone to live with us at the center of their lives catering to all our preferences.

A boundary is not only geographic or physical. It can be a limit we establish which we will not allow others to cross without significant consequences. Boundaries can be behavioral, relational, emotional, or spiritual limits we require with people with whom we choose to have a meaningful relationship. For example, we might choose not to endure emotional abuse by someone's controlling behavior. We might decline to co-sign a note for a good friend, because we either cannot afford to pay the debt or we suspect that the person might be financially unreliable.

A boundary can also be a limitation we place on our own behavior to keep us physically safe or emotionally secure. For example, we might check out the crime rate in a neighborhood before renting an apartment. If the crime rate is higher than we think reasonable, we might rent elsewhere. We could establish a zero tolerance on our consumption of alcohol as a beverage, because we recognize that we do not have good self-control in this area. These choices in boundaries stem from our personal values.

A need to develop stronger boundaries might be present when we feel the need to protect ourselves from ideas with which we do not agree, or when we must criticize or attack people who look at things differently. We might feel inadequate to defend our position or be unwilling or incapable of hearing something we oppose. When someone is drawn primarily to people who are similar and who agree with them on many topics, that person might have a lack of differentiation due to poor boundaries.

We also must recognize and respect the boundaries other people have for how they desire people to relate to them. We approach them on terms they put in place. It is important to listen to others and observe their body language in order to learn their relational preferences. While some people have clear boundaries, they sometimes lack assertiveness to insist that these boundaries be respected by others. It is our responsibility to communicate our boundaries to others. Our mutual respect of other's boundaries and their respect for ours sets the tone for an emotionally healthy relationship.

The Dangers of Enmeshment

A common problem in troubled relationships occurs when one person invades the boundaries of another. One form of this emotional dysfunction is called enmeshment. Enmeshment always connects two or more things together but often in an unhealthy way, because no clear boundary is known or respected by one or both parties. Either they let people control them or they attempt to dominate other people. Both of these extremes bring destruction to relationships.

Enmeshment is the state of being entangled with someone or something. For example, a person can be enmeshed with a friend, an individual with a spouse, or a coach with his team players. Either a boss or an employee can be enmeshed with the other. Enmeshment can sometimes be found between a son and his mother or also become a part of a daughter's relationship with her father. Some people assert adolescent crushes between two teenagers can be a form of enmeshment. Enmeshment refers to the nature of the relationship as a whole. It cannot be assessed by observing a single event, but can be discerned over time when there is an unhealthy bonding of emotional dependence.

Enmeshment can take on many forms. It can be in only one direction. A person can form an enmeshed relationship with a healthy person—at least for a while. But when both persons are enmeshed with each other, a healthy relationship will be virtually impossible. In considerably dysfunctional relationships, enmeshment is often recognized or at least unacknowledged by one person and sometimes both parties. A person also can be enmeshed with an organization with which he significantly identifies and promotes his values. This can take place with almost any type of organization: a school, law firm, church, club, restaurant, or any operation that draws great attention from the person or reinforces one's own false identity or narcissism. This dysfunction is often framed within the context of seemingly healthy, appropriate actions such as love, self-sacrifice, and helping others. But such actions are virtuous only if they rise out of true freedom to do otherwise.

In certain situations, however, enmeshment might occur without any conscious feeling of obligation. For example, an adult child who spends a great deal of time with their parents, eats many of their meals with his parents, and has no savings or health insurance might be a part of an enmeshed family. There is no obvious problem, because everyone gets along well with one another. Although he might be earning part of his own financial support, the adult child does not plan for the future. He can buy the big screen TV he wants, the latest cell phone, and clothes he wants, but he looks to their parents to rescue him financially and emotionally as needed. This is not living as an adult; it is living the life of an adolescent. He has not separated from his parents. He still sees himself under parental provision and protection. This person is still receiving something as a consequence of his intertwinement with his parents. At a minimum, it will be a feeling of being special or feeling particularly good about one's self. A felt compulsion to comply with the other person's agenda is not always a prerequisite for enmeshment, especially when the patterns of emotional and financial dependency have long been in place.[2]

The enmeshed person always gets something as a consequence of this dysfunction. Enmeshment can appear to offer us a sense of security. It can cause us to feel emotionally close to the other person or particularly good about ourselves. This is often mistakenly confused with intimacy and can even be one-sided in a relationship. Of course, along with getting something, we lose something. For example, when we lift someone up onto an emotional pedestal, we become blinded to their faults and sometimes even their strengths, even if that person tries to disclose his true nature. Our emotional fusion with that person distorts our perceptions. When someone feels smothered by an undifferentiated person, they sometimes respond by emotionally disconnecting from that person to assert their personal identity. A discussion of disconnection will follow in the next chapter.

As we grow to form clear individual, personal boundaries, enmeshment with others will sometimes diminish or might go away altogether. People who are maturing emotionally eventually learn to move into non-enmeshed relationships. Enmeshment no longer appeals to them, because they feel anchored to their own personal value system, rather than the values of the person with whom they had been dependent. But when enmeshment does not dissipate, we live with others overly connected with us—or worse yet as one person. In that case, what the other person does is often perceived by us as a reflection upon ourselves. This way of relating will produce many areas of conflict and may result in judgments toward the other person when they do or say something independent of our own personal preferences. When they operate independently from us,

---

2. Ibid., 31.

sometimes our feelings can be easily hurt. To address these issues, we must examine both our feelings and our behavior.

Emotions are Important Cues

Recognizing our negative emotional responses to people can be an indication our boundaries are not respected by others. Of course, not all negative feelings stem from enmeshment. But, we can examine whether or not they do or do not. Emotions are not a sign of weakness. They are an incredible gift from God. Emotions we experience normally tell us something important. Many feelings can be warning signs that we need to do something.[3] For example, fear might tell us to move away from something dangerous. Sadness can tell us we have lost something important to us. Unless we decide to continue living in our sadness, we begin to change something in our life to move away from the sadness. Like fear, anger can signal danger, but instead of withdrawing, anger is sometimes a sign we need to move forward to confront the threat.[4] One such example was Jesus' outrage of the chaos and disrespect going on inside the Temple, which caused him to drive out the abusive money-changers and merchants, so it could return to being a house of prayer.[5] Properly channeled anger can sometimes move us to restore justice in an unjust situation.

Many people are not risk-takers because of emotional fears or past scars. They can strive to control not only their feelings, but also their circumstances to avoid these fears. This can be revealed by addictive behaviors, such as exhibited by alcoholics or workaholics. They mistakenly believe if they control their behaviors (and sometimes those around them) they will not have to face the fears that construct the isolation in which they live.

Positive feelings of love, gratitude, compassion, and joy also tell us important things about our lives. They can help us know who

---

3. Ibid., 159.
4. Ibid., 116.
5. John 2:13-17.

loves us and who we love. Feelings should never be ignored, but they should not be relied upon as the only barometer of health in our relationships.[6] Feelings are important indicators of our desires and preferences, but they are only one element of our internal values.

Enmeshed Behavior

As an enmeshed person, we live overly tied to those people or things. We have an emotional fusion with the other person or thing. It is virtually impossible to see oneself as separate from the other person or thing. We might not do the things we see the other person do, but we are not critical of them. Who they are and what they think and feel will usually reflect what we think and feel.

Identifying the strong foothold of enmeshment can be challenging, because some of the enmeshed responses toward another person could look identical to intentional responses to a person out of unselfish love we might have for them. Both can appear virtuous. The distinctions between authentic, loving actions and enmeshment can best be discerned through the motivations we have for the actions. Pleasing someone we care about is admirable, but if saying "no" causes us anxiety or we feel we have no choice, we might be enmeshed with the other person. Enmeshed people often go out of their way to sacrifice their own needs to do things for others out of a sense of compulsion. Self-centered and controlling people have learned how to manipulate others to get them to do what they want. They see others as an extension of their own self. For the person enmeshed with another, limited emotional freedom exists. The relationship exhibits some level of emotional fusion and behavioral dysfunction. In some ways, the enmeshed person operates as if tied to the other person, rather than as one of two distinct entities. This fusion will ultimately negatively affect both people. Individuality is not properly respected.

---

6. Cloud and Townsend, *Boundaries*, 42.

Here are several examples of behavior that may occur in the midst of enmeshment. If it is with our spouse, we might choose to do what he or she enjoys every Friday night, even if it is not particularly interesting to us while at the same time having fear about disclosing our true feelings. If it is with the firm where we work, we will frequently sacrifice our individual interests for the good of the company. Such sacrifice might mean we work hours and days beyond what we agreed even when others around us do not make the same sacrifices, honestly believing the organization will not be able to operate successfully without our personal sacrifice. If we are enmeshed with a friend, we need their affirmation so much that we will neglect our own personal needs to do things for or with them, even when we know the commitment would not be reciprocal.

The enmeshed person can usually tie their behavior to a virtuous motivation, even when that value is irrelevant to the pressure he or she feels. For example, a doctor, a lawyer, an accountant, or an auto mechanic might regularly sacrifice their private life by working many weekends when others in their operation do not. Their sacrifice is a virtue in their own minds, while others look with amazement at what they so freely give up. Such tendencies might be indicative of a workaholic personality. They can also be a means of avoiding conflict or pain in one's personal life, in spite their belief that their actions are virtuous.

The principles that an enmeshed family employ are often defended with an indisputable principle which appears noble. This principle actually has nothing to do with the real reason they operate as they do. In an enmeshed family, the virtuous, stated value might be "family first." The practice within this family will be that decisions are made for the benefit of the group. Individual needs and desires are sacrificed for what is most desirable for the family. It would be considered disloyal for a member to miss a family gathering because they want to attend a concert with friends. If the family need is for a sense of togetherness which brings about a week-long family vacation, it does not matter whether the individuals have the time, money, or emotional energy to participate; the expectation is for each person to participate. A vacation is organized, even if the expenses for it are not affordable within the family budget. Countless decisions are made to please the majority and individual choices are not encouraged or supported. There are times within a family when it is healthy to make decisions for the good of the group. It becomes problematic where there is no balance between individual and group needs. This can happen when the individual's needs are completely ignored or when "the good of the family" is used in a manipulative way. This behavior is particularly widespread when the family has an autocratic head of household.

In all these enmeshed relationships, we are likely to behave as if our individual needs are not important to us. We are stuck in a pattern that ascribes our value as a person primarily to what we do for others or sometimes for God. A careful examination of our motives can give us a clue as to whether our behavior is initiated out of a sense of compulsion or obligation or is a choice freely made by us to help the other person. If it is out of obligation, we might need to reframe our motives or behavior. It is through looking deeper or from a different perspective that we might discover a source of motivation of which we are not aware. Remember, the condition of enmeshment does not always have to relate to conscious awareness of obligation. We can simply feel good about the enmeshment. Enmeshment may continue even after we cease getting our emotional needs met by the relationship. Sadly, the deeply enmeshed person often lacks the needed objectivity to accurately assess the presence of this dysfunction. A reliable assessment will likely need to come from someone outside our normal sphere of influence.

Enmeshed with God

One of the most revealing signs of enmeshment is an unhealthy connection of one person with another. The enmeshed person does not see a clear line of identity separation with the one with whom he or she is enmeshed. Enmeshment is usually with another person that the person knows, but we can actually become enmeshed with God. This happens when we come to believe that our judgments and those of God are the same. In the same way that enmeshment is a counterfeit to intimacy with other people, it can also be a false intimacy with God. Intimacy with God requires that we recognize and live by appropriate boundaries with God.

The New Testament frequently refers to Christians living in union with Christ. Theologian David Rightmire writes,

> For Paul, union with Christ results in the personal appropriation of the effects of Jesus' life, death, resurrection, and glorification. By sharing in these events, the believer experiences them as living realities. In this way, Christ comes to live in and through a person."[7]

Being in union does not mean that God and we have merged our individuality. Instead, we are the recipients of the benefits of his sacrificial work on our behalf. We are to live in unity with God. God does not reshape his character or behavior to conform to who we are. The unity of the Father, Son, and Holy Spirit does not mean the Persons have merged their individuality.[8] The subject of authentic unity and counterfeit unity will be discussed later in this chapter.

Enmeshment with God is a powerful, unyielding, sometimes embedded spiritual dysfunction. Just as in our interpersonal relationships, this enmeshed relationship with God will be framed as a virtuous way of living. The fusion of someone to God may falsely embolden them with super-confidence regarding their discernment of God's will for themselves and others. Some people will attribute

---

7. R. David Rightmire is a professor of historical theology at Asbury University. The quote above was accessed November 6, 2013, https://www.asbury.edu/academics/departments/christian-studies-philosophy/faculty-staff/david-rightmire,.

8. The Holy Spirit reveals what followers of God through Christ need in order to walk with God. See an expanded discussion on this topic in *Radical Worship: What Sunday Morning Can Never Give You* by Larry D. Ellis, (Denver, Colorado: Adoration Publishing Company, 2014), 65-58.

the ideas they have and words they speak as direct messages from God. There is no need for discussion of a dissenting perspective, because "a view contrary to God's" has little or no merit.

For example, when a pastor is overworking in his or her ministry, the spouse can feel as if they are competing with God and the church for time and attention. If this criticism is framed by the pastor as interference with "the Lord's work," this can result in a great deal of guilt or resentment by the spouse and a defensive attitude by the pastor, who is simply doing what the pastor believed was his or her calling from God. In addition, there can be other problems. T. A. Boyd writes,

> A tension usually exists if a pastor seeks to pastor his or her own family, as this typically presents an enmeshment of roles. Finding a stable and trustworthy extrafamilial support system to depend upon can be a difficult task for the spouse.[9]

When the spouse of a pastor feels alone, he or she can develop resentment against the pastor, the church, and God. The spouse will often find a friend or a support system that is completely disconnected from the influence of the pastor and their church. This action, under these circumstances, may lay the foundation for disconnection by the spouse from the pastor and the organization with which the pastor is perceived enmeshed. Both the enmeshment of the pastor with the church and the withdrawal of the spouse from the relationships can cause pain as emotional distance grows between the pastor and the spouse.

Enmeshment with God is by no means limited to pastors or others in church leadership. Many men and women instruct their families and friends about what they believe God has spoken to them. Using language such as "God told me…" leaves no room for discussion of points of view that differ from their own. After all,

---

9. T. A. Boyd, "Clergy, Personal and Family Issues," in *Baker Encyclopedia of Psychology & Counseling*, ed. David G. Benner and Peter C. Hill (Grand Rapids, MI: Baker Books, 1999), 209.

who will speak against God's plans? This type of enmeshment with God precludes having adult conversations with others and isolates the enmeshed person from the benefit of an abundance of counselors.[10] God gives us the ability to make choices and with freedom of choices comes differentiation and individuality. When God's will is announced in only an absolute way, there is no room for differing beliefs on subjects where historic Christians have not had unanimity. At that point, such absolutism become problematic. Our own loss of objectivity can become equated with God's desires.

Some corporate executives desire to base their business practices on Christian-based values. These people can also fall prey to enmeshment with God. Problems of favoritism toward those whose Christian beliefs are like their own can breed discontentment among the rest of the staff. Fortunately, many admirable business owners desire to conduct their businesses with integrity. They base their business ethics on values clearly stated in the Scriptures. The Scriptures express guiding principles regarding keeping one's word, the benefits of counsel, managing a business with a balanced family life, leadership, hiring and firing decisions, decisions related to borrowing and lending money, partnerships, and retirement. These should be prized values.

Author and teacher Larry Burkett has written over seventy books, many of which address biblical principles of money management and business acumen.[11] He presents a helpful perspective on these subjects, although the reader should carefully assess each suggestion to determine if his perspectives apply to one's own particular situation. Striving to live one's life and operate one's business in alignment with the teachings of Scripture and other positive values is not, in itself, an indication of enmeshment with God. Embracing this value can simply mean one is faithful. As with all enmeshment, it becomes a problem when we feel internally pressured to do things

---

10. Prov 15:22, 11:14.
11. Larry Burkett, *Business by the Book: Biblical Principles for the Workplace* (Nashville, TN: Thomas Nelson, 1998).

a certain way and we yield to that, even though God might prefer a different course of action.

Healthy spirituality includes discerning God's will for us. But, enmeshment takes root when one begins thinking and believing he or she is consistently and accurately aligned with God. Fusion is almost always unconscious on the part of the one who is enmeshed. The dysfunction is not from God's side. Rather, it is present when we project upon God our own preferences and perspectives, and we then attribute them to God. A sign of enmeshment with God can be an inability to listen rationally to perspectives with which we disagree. For example, certain theological perspectives are viewed differently by many Christians. Such perspectives might include the role of the husband or wife in marriage, consumption of alcohol as a beverage, the use of firearms, Christian education of children, the level of authority afforded to our reading of Scripture, the significance of the sacraments of baptism and communion, the Christian perspective on financial debt, the role of women in pastoral leadership in the church, supernatural spiritual gifts, and political views, and especially the appropriate role government should play in our lives. When we discount without discussion the positions of others which differ from our own and at the same time boldly attribute our positions to God's position, we are on dangerous ground and possibly enmeshed with God. While this enmeshment might be more observable when the person is an extrovert with a strong persuasive personality, it can also be quietly lived out by the introverted, ostensibly meek person through passive-aggressive or secret actions never intended for public exposure. The discussion of enmeshment with God will be further expanded in the chapter entitled the Distortion of Authority.

Counterfeit Unity

Uniformity is sameness in manner or form—colors that are exact matches with each other or two people whose ideas on a subject are identical. In contrast, unity is fundamentally different things operating in harmony with each other. Enmeshment is uniformity and counterfeit unity. The most dangerous counterfeit is something that so strongly resembles the real thing that it will be confused with the authentic original. Monopoly money will never be confused with real money, because it does not resemble authentic printed currency. But, the Leaf Scorpionfish is a fish that disguises itself as a piece of colorful, harmless coral or leaf. At first site, it appears inconsequential. However, it is carnivorous and can attack unsuspecting prey such as crab, shrimp, and small fish in milliseconds. Sometimes those things that pose the greatest threat to us do not appear suspicious to us. Because enmeshment is such a thing, we must learn how to discern it in ourselves and others.[12]

In Christian circles, enmeshment can take on a religious flare. For example, a Christian family might appear loving and generous, while at the same time be violating God's foundational principles of forgiveness or living generously. They may simply be loving because they believe being a Christ-follower mandates this, while at the same time continuing their prejudice against others due to race, level of education, or social background. Their external behavior might well not reflect the internal, judgmental attitude of their heart. A penetrating question can be who they avoid, because they have not forgiven that person. Others might be why someone condemns someone with judgments and refuses to help when they have the ability to do so, or why they refuse to admit their wrong doing in their personal life while teaching of virtuous living at church. Such incongruent behavior is actually a poor counterfeit of the true love of God, which is the distinguishing character of Christ-followers.[13]

The Bible can even be used to defend behavior that undermines and destroys relationships. Some Christians would say, "The Bible

---

12. Anna Lynn, "Enmeshment and the Kingdom of God." *Thoughts by AnnaLynn*, May 4, 2013, accessed 11/1/2016, https://thoughtsbyannalynn.wordpress.com/.
13. Ibid.

teaches that women should be subordinate to men." These people might look at the chronology of man being created prior to women and infer some sense of a supervisory role of men over women, even though such an inference is not promoted in the Scriptures. In support of that idea, they quote Genesis 2:18: "Then the Lord God said, 'It is not good that the man be alone; I will make him a helper fit for him.'" A helper, in our traditional understanding in English, relegates a women to be an assistant or even a domestic helper. The Hebrew noun for helper, *ezer*, actually "signifies the action of someone who saves another from extremity, who delivers from death."[14] While this word is used for women in this verse as well as in verse twenty, it is used many times elsewhere in the Old Testament, and in all cases referring specifically to God as redeemer.[15] With this knowledge, rather than evoking a subservient role, we actually understand the opposite. Her presence with man is redemptive and whole-making. To promote female submission as a scriptural teaching elevates men and demotes women from the created order designed by God.

The gospel of John records these words of Jesus, "A new commandment I give to you, that you love one another: just as I have loved you, you also are to love one another. By this all people will know that you are my disciples, if you have love for one another" (John 13:34-35). According to Jesus, this lifestyle of loving one another as Jesus did marks one as a true Christ-follower. One's orthodox (right) beliefs are important, but insufficient to fulfill God's desired transformation of us. At this point, Jesus is shifting the disciples' understanding about what will be the foundation for how people know they are his disciples. He is introducing a paradigm shift from ways of loving in the past to loving one another as he had loved them.

The powerful image of Jesus washing the feet of his disciples speaks to the love and humility with which we are to relate to one

---

14. Manfred T. Brauch, *Abusing Scripture* (Downers Grove, Il: InterVarsity Press, 2009), 125-126.
15. Exod 18:4; Deut 33:7, 26, 29; Ps 33:20; 46:1; 115:9-11,

another today.[16] This new way was apparently unfamiliar to them. Many of these new ways of loving were taught by Jesus in the Sermon on the Mount.[17] Loving one's enemies, being merciful, and feeling blessed because of being persecuted for doing the right thing were not a part of their vision of loving others. These responses went against the cultural tendencies in those days, just as they do today.

Retribution, or getting what one deserves, was not only embedded in the civil culture; it was central to the Jewish culture. Theologian Mark A. Jolley writes, "With the law as its foundation, the history of Israel was a continuous cycle of making retribution. Even in the narrative of Cain and Abel, Cain is punished by being forced to leave his home (Gen 4). All the earth is punished by a devastating flood for widespread sin (Gen 6–9)."[18] Jesus reframed our lives from being measured against the law to being forgiven because of his gracious gift of himself. We are to love one another as Jesus loved and be wary of persuasive counterfeit love. Jesus' love was selfless. He repeatedly served the needs of others, living a life of self-sacrifice. The apostle Paul exhorted the Christians in Philippi to

> Do nothing from selfish ambition or conceit, but in humility count others more significant than yourselves. Let each of you look not only to his own interests, but also to the interests of others. Have this mind among yourselves, which is yours in Christ Jesus, who, though he was in the form of God, did not count equality with God a thing to be grasped, but emptied himself, by taking the form of a servant, being born in the likeness of men. And being found in human form, he humbled himself by becoming obedient to the point of death, even death on a cross. (Phil 2:3-8)

---

16. John 13:1-10.
17. Matt 5-7.
18. Marc A. Jolley, "Retribution," in *Eerdmans Dictionary of the Bible,* ed. David Noel Freedman, Allen C. Myers, and Astrid B. Beck (Grand Rapids, MI: W.B. Eerdmans, 2000), 1122.

Counterfeit unity with God can be rooted in enmeshment with God and enmeshment with other people who are in full agreement with us, but who are living contrary to God's disclosed will. The authentic unity that God seeks in his followers is not simply an agreeable consensus with one another, but an agreeable consensus with God's revealed character and a lifestyle that shows to those outside the faith what God is like, especially by our love for one another.

Resistance Is Not Futile

When we are enmeshed with another person, we are not able to distinguish our ideas, opinions, and values from the person with whom we are overly connected. We tend to cooperate with the other person even when in ourselves we might not want to. If our own values are not developed to a mature level, we might happily defer to the other person, because we fear looking at things differently. The consequences of enmeshment for adults can be quite disempowering, resulting in disappointment and a sense of loss of personal freedom. We recognize enmeshment within ourselves by looking at what we do and resist doing in our relationships. If we tend to avoid expression of our own opinions and follow the lead of the other person without a reasonable assessment, that behavior could be an indication of our lack of independence. If we find ourselves anxious and avoid voicing what we desire, believe, or think with someone, this, too could be an indication of our enmeshment with them.

We can take steps to move away from enmeshment, but such a change will likely present challenges. When someone begins to move away from enmeshment with another person who is enmeshed with him or her, that person can likely expect resistance from the other person. The emotional system in place will become upset and unstable. Because the unhealthy person likes the enmeshment and has been enjoying compliance with their own desires and preferences, the change will be threatening and unwelcome. Recall that we can expect conflict to increase, because the one working toward differentiation is no longer functioning as one half of a single identity. The stronger the steps taken toward independent living, the more conflict will arise. In most situations, as a person strives to individuate and to differentiate, eventually the relational system between the people will begin to adjust to the changes. As enmeshment diminishes, the relationship will ultimately become more healthy. While it is unrealistic to expect an immediate transformation of anyone, the individual seeking the changes becomes strengthened in their ability to assert their boundaries. Fortunately, relational boundaries are not always permanent walls. In fact, we are better served when they are reasonably and intentionally flexible, because when circumstances change, so can some boundaries we have put in place.[19]

---

19. Cloud and Townsend, *Boundaries*, 23.

Chapter 3

The Debilitation of Disconnection

The Nature of Disconnection

Sometimes as we try to move away from enmeshment, we can overreact, moving to distance ourself to a point where we are disconnected from someone. In many cases, when someone strives to become independent from someone with whom they have become enmeshed, the first reactionary step might be disconnection. Many counselors also refer to this as detachment. Disconnection can result from other circumstances, such as an inability to relate well with others or a disproportionate level of insecurity. Disconnection is essentially a severing of a relationship, reflecting a decision to no longer be open to the roles of initiation or response to repair a broken relationship. Disconnected people often justify their own boundary problems by focusing on the bad behavior of the one who has offended them.

The decision to disconnect may be easily justified when a person carries unresolved judgments against another person. When the ongoing wounding is so painful, the need to stop the pain by severing the relationship becomes the primary goal, instead of repairing the relationship. People can make the decision to disconnect out of fear, either real or imagined, of what might become disclosed, should everyone know what actually happened. There might also be a fear of being engulfed, swamped, humiliated, or lost, if the relationship was allowed to continue. They see no alternative in their effort to rid themselves of this problem in the relationship. Sometimes people frame disconnection as a defensive move to cope with relational pain. They hope this move will protect them from ongoing stress.

Disconnection can present itself in subtle ways. It is not always blatantly announced with a big fanfare. We might simply begin to ignore the other person. Their emails and phone calls are simply not returned, but there is no pronouncement of the severed relationship. Some people take this passive-aggressive approach without being crass. They hope that the other person will eventually cease interacting with them. This behavior might lessen the burden on the person detaching.

If someone feels so smothered by the other that acceptance requires denial of their personhood, disconnection may appear the only way forward. They avoid them; they no longer initiate with them. If they meet with significant resistance in their separation process, they sometimes go so far as to cut themselves off entirely from the other person. The individual seeking to establish a boundary sometimes terminates an ongoing relationship with the other person, because they believe the person creates an unmanageable problem for them. When a disconnection is in play, the relationship can no longer lead to strong friendship and intimacy.

The Action of Disconnection

There are many things that can tempt people to disconnect from a person with whom they were once close. If a husband makes his work a higher priority than his relationship with his wife, she can feel he has disconnected with her, and this loss may lead her to find connected relationships elsewhere. If parents do not demonstrate respect for a teen's growing need for personal boundaries and are consistently questioning them on every issue, the young person will likely share less and less of his or her personal life with the parent. That disconnection can sometimes create feelings of great loss for a parent, especially when the parent is enmeshed with the child. While teenagers might not know the term enmeshment, they can usually sense the invasive behavior by others, especially parents, and react against it.

As a short-term detachment, teachers can send misbehaving students to the principal for discipline. This gets the problem student out of the classroom at least temporarily. Society seeks to disconnect those convicted of crimes from the rest of society by placing them into prison. When we feel afraid, deeply offended, or emotionally wounded, we may seek relief by separating ourselves emotionally from that person or culture. Of course, isolation will ultimately further undermine the fabric of those strained relationships, especially when we must continue to relate to these people such as family members and others with whom we live and work. In certain circumstances, disconnection can seem to restore a level of order through temporary relief from stressful relationships, but there will be a cost for this choice. Reconciliation cannot take place. There will be no renewal of a healthy relationship.

Disconnection is often used as a defense mechanism, a way to cope with relational pain. Severing the relationship is thought to remove the pain. It does not. While it is often a conscious choice, disconnection can also be an unconscious action in direct response to the strained relationship. Even though a tendency toward disconnection usually presents itself as a cutoff from a few specific people, an individual might see this approach as a solution to many conflicted relationships. This tendency to disconnect in an attempt to avoid conflict will make it difficult for others to become connected to such a person.

Disconnection can sometimes be separation by physical distancing. More often, disconnection places an intentional, emotional distance between people. Disconnected people are emotionally cut-off from others. They sometimes appear to have a serious communication problem, but actually the lack of communication is more a symptom of a problem than the underlying problem of emotional unavailability. When we successfully address and resolve what is causing the person to isolate themselves, we can expect communications to improve.[1] Just as the formation of disconnection is commonly an active decision, there must also be specific actions to reconnect.

The Restoration from Disconnection

A therapist once told me "the only way out of pain is through it." She meant the way to reclaim health in a broken relationship is to willingly step into the pain and examine why and how we came into the situation. In relationships, that decision means we must continue to relate to that person, if possible, hopefully in a healthier way. If we withdraw completely from a relationship, we have taken the one sure way to ensure that healing will never be restored. The best treatment for our disconnection from someone is usually learning how to become better differentiated. The foundation of good differentiation is our establishing and living with good boundaries that we put in place.

Distinctions between Disconnection and Differentiations

Disconnection should not be confused with the normal, healthy process of differentiation. Sometimes people do not clearly see the distinctions between disconnection and a differentiated relationship. The thing that both have in common is that they are not overly dependent upon other people. Unfortunately, the disconnected person lives with the polar opposite dysfunction of one who is enmeshed with another person. Rather than being overly connected with someone, the disconnected person strives to avoid any meaningful relationship with the person. An attempt at disconnection can sometimes be seen following a divorce when an ex-wife refers to "the children's father" rather than referring to him by his name. A person

---

1. Roberta M. Gilbert, *Extraordinary Relationships: A New Way of Thinking about Human Interactions* (New York: John Wiley & Sons, Inc., 1992), 104.

can be radically disconnected from the other person, often living in reaction to the other person's behavior. In contrast, the differentiated person has a balanced life enjoying a reasonable connection with others, but is not fused with them. Being differentiated does not mean there are no crises in their relationship. Instead, one's relationship is maintained in spite of any shortcoming that both people bring to their relationship. The differentiated person is neither disconnected nor enmeshed.

Differentiation will be discussed in detail in chapter 4, but the result of differentiation will be a healthy balance between being separate from others and being connected to them in a healthy manner. Disconnection is an inadequate, counterfeit substitute for differentiation. Like counterfeit money, it provides no authentic medium of exchange between people. Many people who are disconnected from others will not see the nuanced, but distinctive, difference between these two conditions. Learning to recognize and engage in a healthy balance between our separateness and togetherness with others is crucial to maintaining emotionally healthy relationships.

Chapter 4

The Surprises about Differentiation

Differentiation Is Being Balanced

A differentiated person understands each of us is a separate entity from the other and values a strong sense of self, but also maintains a healthy balance between separateness and togetherness with other people. The natural consequence of differentiation is diversity. In this chapter, I will examine how this balance within God's creative process, as recorded in the Scriptures, provides the foundation of our union of diversity, rather than uniformity in all God has designed and created.

God Is Differentiated from All Else

Theologian David Dockery writes, "God is personal and is differentiated from other beings, nature, and the universe. This contrasts with current philosophical approaches to God that say God is in a part of the world, creating a continual process, and the process itself is the actuality."[1] The Scriptures describe attributes of God that stand against the thinking that God is creating a continual process.[2]

---

1. David S. Dockery, Trent C. Butler, et al., *Holman Bible Handbook* (Nashville, TN: Holman Bible Publishers, 1992), 811.
2. For readers who do not view the Scriptures as authoritative, the author recommends the following books for consideration: *The Blue Parakeet: Rethinking How You Read the Bible* by Scot McKnight (Grand Rapids, MI: Zondervan, 2008) and *Whose Bible is It?* by Jaroslav Pelikan (New York, NY: Penguin Books, 2005).

This popular but flawed understanding critiqued by Dockery postulates God as being in flux and changing as part of the cosmic process, seeing God and valuing him for what he was and will become. The reality is God's character and personality are not evolving. He does not change and learn from his interaction with his creation. The steadfast faithfulness of God does not change.

The Old Testament prophet Malachi wrote "I am the Lord, and I do not change" (Mal 3:6).[3] The New Testament writer James wrote, "Every good gift and every perfect gift is from above, coming down from the Father of lights with whom there is no variation or shadow due to change" (Jas 1:17). God is the same as he always has been and will be. The Scriptures reveal God as spirit.[4] He is alive,[5] actively working,[6] intelligent,[7] intentional and acts with purpose,[8] and is fully autonomous.[9] Because God is a free agent; his actions are determined solely by his own nature and pleasure.

Only an absolutely free person can limit himself, and God has chosen to limit himself. In his human form, Jesus could only be in one place at a time. He endured physical discomforts of pain and hunger. He submitted to a grueling physical death. In addition, God will not do anything prohibited by his own nature. Because God is personal, he is self-aware and knows himself fully.[10] He experiences and expresses emotions; yet these emotions, unlike some humanly expressed emotions, are not mixed with imperfections or weaknesses. From the Scriptures, we discover some of his emotions. He

---

3. Tyndale House Publishers, *Holy Bible: New Living Translation* (Carol Stream, IL: Tyndale House Publishers, 2013).
4. John 4:24.
5. Deut 5:26.
6. John 5:17.
7. Rom 11:33.
8. Eph 1:11; 3:11.
9. Ps 135:5-9.
10. Exod 3:14.

loves,[11] shows compassion,[12] shows joy and delight,[13] expresses anger,[14] demonstrates pity,[15] is jealous,[16] and can suffer and be grieved by events and people's actions.[17]

Scripture also reveals God lives with us as individuals as well as within the community of Christ-followers.[18] The Holy Spirit lives with us. We do not contain God, nor do we become God in any sense. God does not fuse himself with us. We cannot fuse ourselves with God, despite the belief of some Christians that their decisions stem from direct revelations from God. As discussed earlier, the Christian's union with Christ speaks to our being the recipient of his gift of himself, not a convergence of humans with God. God always remains distinct and separate from humanity, yet he is always drawn to us because of his love for us. In theological terms, he is transcendent (separate, distinct, away from us), while he is also immanent (close to us and present in our midst.) He is neither enmeshed nor disconnected from us. He is fully differentiated from us, distinct from all his creation. Yet, he connects with us while never surrendering his separateness from us.

God Divides

God is often understood primarily as one who unites people. Like many ideas, this is partially true, but without further examination, this statement is potentially misleading. Do not mistake uniformity (being alike) with unity. The virtuous unity we are

---

11. Deut 7:7-8, Isa 43:4, Jer 31:13, Hos 11:1, Mark 10:21, John 3:16, John 13:1, John 17:28, and 1 John 4:8,10,19.
12. Ps 103:13; Exod 33:19, Deut 13:1, Judg 2:18, Ps 116:5, Ps 145:8, Matt 9:36, Matt 14:14, Matt 15:32, Matt 20:34, and Mark 8:2.
13. Jer 32:41, Isa 62:4-5, and Luke 15:32.
14. Exod 22:34, Deut 6:14-15, Jer 7:20, Ezra 5:13, Matt 21:12-13, Mark 11:15-17, Luke 19:45-46, and John 2:14-17.
15. Ps 103:3.
16. Deut 6:14-15.
17. Luke 24:46-47, John 6:51; 10:11; 11:50-52, and 1 Pet 2:21-24; Gen 6:6; John 11:35.
18. Acts 6:5, 1 Cor 6:19, and 2 Cor 6:16.

to have in our human relationships stems from his people living together in harmony with God's agendas, not simply agreement with those around them regarding their desires. The powerful cohesive harmony of great music is possible only when singing and playing in unison is exchanged for a harmony of notes and rhythms played according to the musical score under the direction of a competent musical leader.

Unity must be clearly distinguished from uniformity. God loves and creates diversity, not uniformity. The starting point for creation was chaos. The second verse of the Bible states, "The earth was without form and void, and darkness was over the face of the deep" (Gen 1:2). The description of "without form and void" could be translated as emptiness or formlessness.[19] Theologian Allen Ross describes the earth at that point; "it was a chaos of wasteness, emptiness, and darkness."[20] At this point in time, the creation was in disorder; it lacked differentiation.

In the first two chapters of the book of Genesis we quickly observe uniformity and chaos are not God's ultimate plan for his creation. Instead, we see the repeated process of differentiation of his creation. We will see God so greatly values differentiation. He models it over and over throughout his creation process. The first example of differentiation is the separation of light and darkness. "And God said, 'Let there be light,' and there was light. And God saw that the light was good. And God separated the light from the darkness. God called the light Day, and the darkness he called Night" (Gen 1:3-5). The second differentiation is the creation of an expanse or space which would separate the water above (precipitation) from the bodies of waters below (oceans).[21] The third was the gathering

---

19. Francis Brown, Samuel Rolles Driver, and Charles Augustus Briggs, *Enhanced Brown-Driver-Briggs Hebrew and English Lexicon* (Oxford: Clarendon Press, 1977), 1062.
20. Allen P. Ross, "Genesis," in *The Bible Knowledge Commentary: An Exposition of the Scriptures,* ed. J. F. Walvoord and R. B. Zuck, vol. 1 (Wheaton, IL: Victor Books, 1985), 28.
21. Gen 1:6-7.

of the waters below which was distinct from the gathering of land.[22] Following the differentiation of land from the seas, God then brought forth vegetation.[23] At this point God has distinguished between inorganic matter and organic life that is of a vegetable nature. Next God distinguished between night and day, creating a dim light for nighttime.

The Differentiation of Humanity

The next differentiation is particularly discriminating. Living plants were separated from sentient beings. God separated the unconscious life of vegetation from conscious animal life. The great living creatures in the sea and those who fly through the sky were created.[24] The seventh differentiation in the creation was the formation of "living creatures according to their kinds—livestock and creeping things and beasts of the earth according to their kinds" (Gen 1:24). Francis Schaeffer reminds us, "At this point, everything has been produced and differentiated with the exception of one thing, and that is humanity. And so we come, finally, to the distinction which is so overwhelmingly important to us. God sets man and woman apart from bare being, vegetable life, and the conscious life of fish, birds and animals."[25] In Genesis 1:26 God states, "Let us make man in our image, after our likeness.[26] And let them have dominion over the fish of the sea and over the birds of the heavens and over the livestock and over all the earth and over every creeping thing that creeps on

---

22. Gen 1:9.
23. Gen 1:11-12.
24. Gen 1:20-21.
25. Francis A. Schaeffer, *The Complete Works of Francis A. Schaeffer: A Christian Worldview*, vol. 2 (Westchester, IL: Crossway Books, 1982), 25–26.
26. Although the Hebrew words for image and likeness are different, there is no connecting conjunction between them. Therefore, the two words do not list differing ideas that must be connected. Instead, both words refer to the same concept, the second, word, likeness, simply reinforces the concept of image.

the earth."[27] Being made in God's image does not mean we contain the essence of God. We do not ever become divine. The Scripture continues in the next verse, "So God created man in his own image, in the image of God he created him; male and female he created them" (Gen 1:27). This makes it clear "man" as used here means humanity and specifically includes both "male and female." Scripture declares both women and men are made in God's image. God entrusted this dominion to both men and women, not just men. This perspective will be discussed further in the next chapter.

Humanity stands in stark contrast to all that has been previously created. Women and men are the only part of creation that are made in the image of God (*imago dei*). Many distinctions through creation reveal the absolute necessity of differentiation required for procreation of God's living creation. Diversity, not uniformity, was God's intention from the onset of creation. The consequence of differentiation is always diversity. Even when there is widespread agreement about one topic, there will remain differences on other subjects and often nuances that create slightly different perspectives. There are certain limits on orthodoxy (right or correct belief) which must not be crossed within the Christian community. These beliefs, however, would primarily relate to the nature of God and Jesus as explicitly revealed in the Scriptures. In countless ways, we are to extend grace to others who have a different understanding on the other topics.

God's preference for diversity, rather than uniformity, can make some Christ-followers uncomfortable. Such persons are most comfortable when everyone operates in the same way—the way they think and believe. This predilection might indicate a distorted understanding of the meaning and role of authority and possibly

---

27. In the Hebrew text from which Genesis is translated the words for image and likeness are different, but there is no conjunction between them in the text. Therefore, we understand the words to mean the same thing. The addition of likeness is there to restate the identical idea of image.

even enmeshment with God. These subjects are discussed further in chapter 7.

Another area of differentiation is put forth in the New Testament; God endows every Christ-follower with at least one spiritual gift. No one person is guaranteed multiple gifts, but it is not unusual for God to give several spiritual gifts to a person. According to the apostle Paul, these special, personal gifts are bestowed by God "to equip the saints for the work of ministry, for building up the body of Christ" (Eph 4:12). Because of this clearly stated purpose, we must not assume these gifts are bestowed to make us proud or to build up our personal esteem. Once again, we see differing strengths empowered by the Holy Spirit bring about a unified advancement of the Kingdom of God on Earth. The challenge is for Christ-followers to enjoy secure acceptance of the many blessings and gifts given to others, without enmeshment, envy, or judgments thus valuing being differentiated and living together in harmony as God intends.

Differentiated relationships are great treasures in our life. The best forms of intimacy can be experienced within these friendships. We develop and offer healthy intimacy only by developing our separateness. There is a mutual respect for each other's boundaries. Differentiated people create a safe space for others to open up and share their confessions of difficulties and failures as well as their joyous events. Confidentiality is secure and judgments are withheld, while honest assessment and advice can be lovingly exchanged.

When we are differentiated, we see ourselves as only responsible for ourselves. We can do things for others, but we do so voluntarily out of appreciation or love, not out of guilt or a sense of compulsion. Being separate means we are responsible to manage our own emotions so they do not bring unnecessary stress into the relationship. It is only when we are differentiated from another person that we can truly love them in an emotionally healthy way. Only with differentiation can there ultimately be unity. It is foundational in how we relate to others. It is not hindered by difference in age, gender, level of education, politics, or theology. It allows us to learn from and about those with whom we do not agree. It frees us to learn to forgive those who hurt us. We are less easily hurt because we are not enmeshed with others.

The Empowerment of Differentiation

Some people might mistakenly think that differentiation is best learned by separating ourselves from other people. However, withdrawal could actually thrust us toward disconnection. Differentiation is exclusively our individual work upon ourselves to improve ourselves. But, differentiation cannot be learned apart from others. It is much like forgiveness of someone who has offended us. Both processes go much more easily if the other person recognizes the problem and takes ownership of what they have done. But your ultimate success both in forgiveness and differentiation rests finally upon our own process of spiritual and emotional growth. As we take full ownership for our own feelings and behavior, we cease to blame others for how we feel and act. The behavior of others becomes almost inconsequential to how we behave.

Differentiation is a spiritual and emotional balance of being able to connect with others and at the same time maintain our own individual identity. A differentiated person is not disconnected from those with whom he disagrees. He can engage with those people, even when the other persons have a tendency to violate his boundaries. A person with a healthy sense of differentiation from others can listen to and understand points of view with which they might not agree without being personally threatened. It is from these types of conversations we can learn a great deal, often more than talking with someone who is in full agreement with us. We can give serious consideration to other perspectives and learn. We might even come to the point of changing our position on some matters. Differentiation is a valuable prerequisite for learning.

Psychiatrist Roberta Gilbert states people are generally drawn to other people who operate at the same level of differentiation they employ. While this might be our preference, it is not always our opportunity to do so. Also, people who are well differentiated are less likely to become stuck in unproductive patterns. She continues:

> At higher levels of differentiation, relationships serve whatever togetherness needs there may be, but since there are fewer togetherness needs, the two tend to function more as a harmonious team. Individuality is never lost in high relationships. Rather, in and throughout all the teamwork, there exist two total and complete individuals, fully aware of self and the other, in open communication with each other. That is the ideal.[28]

Healthy relationships need a level of connection accompanied with a certain level of independence. When both states are lived out in a healthy, balanced way, the person is differentiated. Being differentiated does not mean the changed relationship is necessarily celebrated by the other person. Living in a differentiated way might well generate additional conflict with someone, but a differentiated person does not assume responsibility for the conflict, even though we recognize and have compassion for the struggle in the other person. The differentiated person resists the entrapments of both enmeshment and disconnection.

From biology, we see a helpful illustration about the importance of differentiation. An undifferentiated cell of a multi-cellular organism can give rise to infinitely more cells of precisely the same type—undifferentiated. They are the basic cells from which all other cells are derived as they mature. Tissues contain stem cells as a reservoir of undifferentiated cells. These cells can change into a wide variety of specialized cells depending upon which of the genes in the common DNA are expressed. As it grows and differentiates, the cell can become what it is designed to ultimately become, such as bone

---

28. Gilbert, *Extraordinary Relationships*, 97.

cells, brain cells, or muscle cells. A cell must differentiate to mature and function.[29]

One of the foundational aspects of relational differentiation is individuation. Individuation is "the process by which individuals in society become differentiated from one another."[30] When we have become individuated (differentiated), we take responsibility for our own positions on matters and speak only for ourselves, never the other person. We also strive not to assume the role of managing other people's emotions for them. An example could be the spouse of an alcoholic attempting to hide the problem from others to keep up a good image for the spouse. We do not assume responsibility for shielding them from the consequences of their choices and actions. We do not carry the stresses of trying to manage things in the other person over which we have no control or responsibility. We focus on how we act toward others in a non-invasive manner.

Moving away from the enmeshment of youth and adolescence or the disconnection which may occur because of a painful past and toward a healthy differentiation is a challenging process. But, as our process of differentiation develops, we will find a new level of independence from people and circumstances that have seemed to control us in the past. We will experience great freedom. We will also take full ownership for decisions we make. Our successful work here will empower us with a sense of emotional liberation.

I provide one word of caution here. It is possible certain long-termed relationships, where enmeshment is deeply rooted and such dysfunction is maintained, can blind us to our unhealthy fusion with others. It is likely, however, as people mature toward differentiated relationships, this new emotional independence will continue to impact many relationships. Fortunately, differentiation

---

29. Catherine Soanes and Angus Stevenson, eds., *Concise Oxford English Dictionary* (Oxford: Oxford University Press, 2004).

30. Frederick C. Mish, "Preface," *Merriam-Webster's Collegiate Dictionary*. (Springfield, MA: Merriam-Webster, Inc., 2003).

eventually becomes second nature to us, especially in newly forming relationships.

To progress into a differentiated lifestyle, we must first embrace that we need to be connected to other people and at the same time maintain our own individual identity. Rather than view this idea as an oxymoron, we can see in Scripture that both the closeness of God to us and the separateness of God from us is the cornerstone of who he is. We are like he is in that sense. All of his creation exhibits differentiation. We can learn to maintain this balance only as we live within a community. We cannot develop differentiation by withdrawing from those who are different from us. Taking complete ownership of ourselves and our own feelings and refusing to take responsibility for the feelings that others have is critical. When we do so, the equilibrium of past relationships will likely become uncomfortable. But as we maintain our ownership of ourselves and avoid the temptation to manage other people's feelings, we will become more confident and see the hope of increased connection begin to appear.

Differentiation implies diversity. The concept of diversity of all God's creation demonstrates his agenda of differentiation. God's intent distinguishes between the inanimate and animate, plant and animal life, low level and high level of intelligent life, and sex. For those who insist that others become like they are, this reality can be troublesome, because this differentiation goes both to the nature of God as Trinity and to the original design of humanity to become a union of diversity within his kingdom. As we embrace differentiation, we can become liberated to also embrace the goodness of all of God's diverse designs.

Chapter 5

God's Design for Humanity

In this chapter, we will examine two elements of God's intentional design for humans. Both of these elements reveal a portion of God's character and what should be the norm for our relationships with one another. First, people are made in the image of God. Second, we are designed to live in unity with one another. Both of these elements are given only to people, not to any other of his many magnificent creations. Healthy personal relationships with one another will best come about as we recognize and live out of these perspectives. It is fascinating how these two seemingly different characteristics are actually intertwined with one another.

Made in the Image of God

The book of Genesis explains it was God's intention that human beings be differentiated from all other living creatures as well as all his inanimate creations. God created us special and to relate to each other and to him in a way no other part of the creation can. As beautiful as the mountains, deserts, plants, and animals are, none of these created objects are made in God's image. They can exhibit God's glory and partially reveal his greatness, but only humans are identified in the Scriptures as being made in God's image. Christ-followers are to reveal the image of God to others as they observe us. Not only do women and men learn we are made in God's image from the book of Genesis, but there are many places where this truth is restated in the New Testament. Speaking about the destruction of the use of the tongue by certain Christians, the author of James writes, "With it we bless our Lord and Father, and with it we curse people who are made in the likeness of God" (Jas 3:9). Speaking to the Christians in Rome about Jesus, the apostle Paul wrote, "For those whom he foreknew he also predestined to be conformed to the image of his Son…" (Rom 8:29).

Theologians have long debated the meaning of being made in God's image. Certainly, we do not physically look like God. Jesus stated God is spirit.[1] An image of something does not become the object it resembles. The viewing of a photograph of someone can give us a partial impression of their physical likeness—an image, but will not be mistaken for the actual person. An image must be distinct from what it resembles. A wedding ring is universally understood as a symbol but not an image of a relationship of love. It cannot be made to look like a relationship. The main purpose of an image is to provide for us an example, demonstration, or understanding of that which it resembles as depicted by the creator.

There are primarily three, somewhat different Christian views of what being made in God's image can mean. The first view teaches we have an endowment. Each person is given certain characteristics that God also possesses. God's image is intrinsically tied up in what makes us human and therefore distinct from all other animals and part of creation. The second view is the popular view that humanity was created to show all of creation what God is like by the way we live our lives. The reformer John Calvin explained this concept with the analogy of a mirror. A mirror reflects the image of what it is pointed toward. The reflection is clear and accurate. When the mirror is not pointed toward the desired object, the desired image is lost. The image of God cannot be seen. Therefore, humans present God's image only to the extent they are in a proper relationship with him.[2] The third view understands the image of God as our purpose for being. It is neither something we possess (an endowment) or

---

1. John 4:24.
2. Stanley J. Grenz, *The Social God and the Relational Self* (Louisville: Westminster John Knox Press, 2001), 166-170.

something we do (an activity), but it is what God designed us to become.[3] As we mature in our knowledge and experience of God, we are transformed to reveal what God's nature is to those who observe us.

Depending upon which view we embrace, the consequences will move us to a particular perspective. However, all of them will teach us we are to live as a part of a supernatural community that manifests the nature and heart of God. As Christ-followers, we understand living as God would have us live with one another is to permeate every dimension of our relationships. We are to live in loving interdependence with one another in the same way that God does through the Trinitarian relationship of the Father, Son, and the Holy Spirit.[4] While we understand God and humanity are not fused, we must acknowledge and take ownership of the uniqueness and responsibilities God has given only to humankind and not provided to any of the rest of his diverse creations.

God Desires Unity

We have seen that the breadth of God's creation reflects diversity on many levels. With diversity, he also desires unity—for us to share the values he has and enjoy love and affection for one another amidst our many differences. Just as God has called Christ-followers to become good stewards of the creation we are blessed to enjoy, he also expects us to take proper, loving care of our relationships with one another. Throughout the gospels, we see how Jesus and his disciples related to one another. In the epistles, the writers of Scriptures frequently discuss the nature of loving relationships within the churches. The best example of unity the Scriptures reveal is the community of the Trinity. We know God is One, but is revealed in three distinct persons, Father, Son, and Holy Spirit, who live with and respect one another. There is unity in the internal love and

---

3. Larry D. Ellis, *Radical Worship: What Sunday Morning Can Never Give You* (Denver, CO: Adoration Publishing Company, 2015), 23-30.
4. Ibid., 31-37.

fellowship within God, as well as differences in the roles each person of the Trinity exercises. The Trinity reflects the perfect relationship. Because God's very nature is relational, as revealed in the Trinity, our very nature as human beings made in his image, is also relational. For this reason, our relationships with one another are important to God. The differentiated relationships within the Trinity are a model for our relationships with one another. The Trinity encompasses diversity in form and mission, living in complete harmony and unity. We are called to live the same way as a part of the community of Christ-followers. Living out of the reality that we are made in God's image means our relationships are to experience and reveal what God is like. As others examine our life and our relationships, we will exhibit the answer to Jesus' prayer to his Father, when he prayed,

> I do not ask for these only, but also for those who will believe in me through their word, that they may all be one, just as you, Father, are in me, and I in you, that they also may be in us, so that the world may believe that you have sent me. The glory that you have given me I have given to them, that they may be one even as we are one, I in them and you in me, that they may become perfectly one, so that the world may know that you sent me and loved them even as you loved me. (John 17:20-24)

As important as right theology is, orthodox teaching will not persuade the world to follow God. Jesus revealed the true solution. The Gospel of John records these words: "By this all people will know that you are my disciples, if you have love for one another" (John 13:36). Experiencing and demonstrating unity of heart and great love for each other will show others the true nature of God. This type of love will be persuasive. Our unity is based on our recognition of God's work adopting us into his family is possible only because of the gift of his Son, not any good deeds we might have accomplished, no matter how significant.

God's Connected Design Elements

As we examined the topics included in this chapter, we discovered two important lessons about how God designed us to live. First, we are like God, in some ways, since he patterned us after who he is. We are made in his image. How we live is to reveal what God is like as others observe how we relate to one another. We are to be the image of God that they see. We are also designed to live in harmony and love with all those who follow Jesus. All followers of Jesus would include many people who understand theology and Christian responsibility differently from how we understand them. Our unity does not stem from sameness, but is foundational in spite of our differences. There is no promise of significant unity with those who are not Christ-followers, even though we are to strive toward that end, just as God does.

Chapter 6

Boundaries Are Biblical

Jesus Set Boundaries

It might come as a great surprise that Jesus set boundaries. Many people think it is rude to tell someone no when they request our time or money. These people might not want to displease anyone. After all, Jesus said, "It is more blessed to give than to receive" (Acts 20:35). The reality is Jesus was not always perceived as nice to people; often he did not do what they wanted.[1]

Jesus was crystal clear about his mission on earth. He did not let conflicting agendas persuade him to operate outside of his intended boundaries. For example, Jesus set a boundary for physical self-protection. When Jesus returned to Nazareth, his home town, as usual he went to the synagogue on the Sabbath. There he read aloud the Scriptures from the book of Isaiah the prophet. Those present enjoyed hearing what pleased them; they were promised deliverance from captivity and blindness. This was welcomed news. They were also agreeable with Jesus declaring that the prophesy he read aloud was fulfilled that very day and that he was the anointed one to bring liberty. But, when he told them things they did not want to hear about God's grace being extended to the Gentiles, they became furious and mobbed him, intending to throw him off a cliff. Jesus pushed through the crowd and fled to safety and continued his ministry. He

---

1. Thanks go to Bill Gaultiere for the research detailing how Jesus frequently set boundaries. Accessed July 1, 2016, www.soulshepherding.org/1998/07/jesus-set-boundaries/.

was focused on his mission and did not need the approval of those in the synagogue to make known their mistaken practices.[2] He maintained his boundaries regarding theological truth as well as those needed for his own physical protection.

Jesus valued solitude and protected it with appropriate boundaries. He withdrew from crowds, sometimes alone and sometimes with friends to reconstitute his peace of mind and pray. Jesus could say no to those who approached him during these times. He utilized a boundary for protection of his time away from the demands of ministry to the public. The gospel of Luke reports after healing a leper, the news about Jesus went abroad and great crowds gathered to hear him preach and to seek physical healing. Luke wrote, "But, he would withdraw to desolate places and pray" (Luke 5:16). The legitimate pressing needs of so many people did not prevent him from taking the respite he needed.

Jesus did not do his ministry alone. Because of the demands of ministry, he consistently drew personal support from others close to him. He was also secure enough to disclose his need for companionship and support with those he loved. Following the Last Supper with his disciples, he went to Gethsemane with them and said, "My soul is very sorrowful, even to death; remain here, and watch with me" (Matt 26:38). He desired personal connection with his disciples.

Jesus said no to inappropriate behavior. He did not submit to an entitlement attitude from those who loved him. Matthew reported, "While he was still speaking to the people, behold, his mother and his brothers stood outside, asking to speak to him. But he replied to the man who told him, 'Who is my mother, and who are my brothers?' And stretching out his hand toward his disciples, he said, 'Here are my mother and my brothers! For whoever does the will of my Father in heaven is my brother and sister and mother'" (Matt 12:46-50). He looked beyond the desires of those who loved him and wanted time with him. He remained focused on the agenda

---

2. Luke 4:16-28.

given to him by his Father, when it would have been easy to favor those who were especially close to him.

Jesus also decided to limit himself from some of the great works he could have done because of people's unbelief.[3] As he was explaining to his disciples that he would be killed and arise on the third day, Peter took him aside and said that would never happen. Jesus rebuked him saying, "Get behind me, Satan! You are a hindrance to me. For you are not setting your mind on the things of God, but on the things of man" (Matt 16:23). Jesus had an unambiguous mission for our redemption and could not be manipulated by Peter's passionate declarations, even though they came from a beloved friend. In the same way, he would not be deterred from his Father's mission for him, getting sidetracked by cynical questions. When religious leaders asked him bating questions, trying to make him look foolish, he had shrewd, insightful questions as responses. When the Pharisees tried to entrap Jesus in order to get him arrested, they asked, "Is it right to pay taxes to Caesar or not?" Jesus called them hypocrites. He asked why there were trying to trap him and whose picture and title are on the coin. Because it was a Roman coin, the image was that of Caesar. Jesus then declared, "Give to Caesar what belongs to Caesar, and give to God what belongs to God" (Matt 22:15-22).

Finally, Jesus offered examples of how we are to set boundaries in our lives. He told us that when we pray, we are to go into a private space and pray to our Father.[4] He taught us we need to set priorities when he said we cannot serve two masters.[5] When he was discussing making false statements, Jesus said we are to answer directly by being honest, direct, and unambiguous. When being accused of making false statements he said we are to answer directly saying either yes or no.[6] Theologian Craig Blomberg writes, "Rather, Jesus' followers should be people whose words are so characterized

---

3. Matt 13:53-58.
4. Matt 6:6.
5. Luke 16:13.
6. Matt 5:37.

by integrity that others need no formal assurance of their truthfulness in order to trust them."[7] He could establish and live by clear boundaries and exhorted his followers to do the same. Jesus was therefore differentiated.

Because Jesus set and lived by a number of intentional boundaries, we will next examine one of his most well-known teachings which will exhibit a number of examples of good and poor boundaries resulting in enmeshment, disconnection, and differentiation. Following that story, the next story is about a courageous confrontation of a powerful king, by a man who had a strong boundary concerning his immediate calling from God, despite the possible consequences. We will then examine a number of other biblical persons who had well-established, clear boundaries. Finally, we will look at several additional prominent leaders and their success with healthy boundaries.

The Man with Two Lost Sons

Luke 15 records a parable that Jesus taught to those who were curious about his teachings.[8] He told the fictional story of a man who had two sons to illustrate several important truths. It is often referred to as the story of the prodigal son. In short, the commonly accepted point of this parable is that a man had a son who was wayward and insisted on being given his inheritance prior to his father's death. His father consented, and this young son went away and squandered all his inheritance. When he came to his senses, in part through hunger and humiliating work, he humbled himself and returned home, hoping for acceptance as a hired hand. Even under those conditions, he would then be better off than in his present state. When he arrived

---

7. Craig Blomberg, *Matthew,* vol. 22, *The New American Commentary* (Nashville: Broadman & Holman Publishers, 1992), 112.
8. A parable is a simple, short story teaching a spiritual or moral lesson. It usually has two different meanings. The first one illustrates the truth about the character or objects in the story. When Jesus used this method of teaching, there was a more important second level that related the truth in the story to a truth about God and his kingdom.

home, his father welcomed him with open arms and even threw a party because of his joy that this wayward son had repented and returned to rejoin the family. This abbreviated version is consistent with the parable, but falls considerably short of the entire scope of what we can learn from this important teaching by Jesus.

The introductory sentence of this parable declares this man had two sons.[9] That element of this parable is quite important, because we can learn as much from the older son's behavior as the younger son's; we also can learn a great deal about the father of these two boys. When the younger son took his money and went away, he disconnected from both his father and his brother. He lived totally on his own in a foreign country, distant from his entire family. He made all his own choices. Jesus gives us no background as to why this younger son chose to cut himself off and separate, but the consequence of that decision was disastrous. He chose not to have the benefits of a loving family nearby and the ongoing provision of his father because he had chosen to withdraw from his family relationships.

The older son had a very different approach to the family system. He did not approve of his younger brother wanting his inheritance early. He also disapproved of his father giving it to him. Because the younger son returned home, the older son could now expect part of his own future inheritance to provide support for his immature, younger brother. The older son had remained home and worked reliably to do all that was needed to help the family business, striving hard to please his father. Despite the fact as the older son, he would receive twice the inheritance his younger brother would receive, he was not happy when his younger brother returned home, having squandered his inheritance and again assumed dependence upon his father's generosity.

When his father saw the younger son approaching from a great distance, he ran to greet his son. He welcomed this son back home.

---

9. Luke 15:11.

The father told the servants, "'Bring quickly the best robe, and put it on him, and put a ring on his hand, and shoes on his feet. And bring the fattened calf and kill it, and let us eat and celebrate. For this my son was dead, and is alive again; he was lost, and is found.' And they began to celebrate" (Luke 15:22-24). When their father announced the coming celebration for the return of his wayward son, the older brother refused to attend the gathering, despite being invited by his father. This son was angry and jealous. He was not pleased by his father's welcome of his foolish brother. When the father asked him to join in the celebration, his response was, "Look, these many years I have served you, and I never disobeyed your command, yet you never gave me a young goat, that I might celebrate with my friends. But when this son of yours came, who has devoured your property with prostitutes, you killed the fattened calf for him" (Luke 15:29-30)! He was angry with his father and his brother. It is interesting that the older son was not only critical of his brother for being wasteful, he accused him of immoral behavior, which he could not have known. The older son believed because he had been the reliable son, his father would love him, perhaps even more than his younger brother. But, the father loved both his sons. His love was not a response to either son's behavior; it was in spite of it. The father even declared all he now had belonged to the older son. The younger son will not receive a second inheritance. The story ends declaring the great love the father had for both sons, but no mention was made of the older son engaging in the celebration with his father, brother, and friends. We have every reason to believe he did not attend the party.

Looking at this story within the framework of our study here, it is obvious the younger son had chosen to fully disconnect from his family. Perhaps that choice was his best attempt at coping with the world and growing into adulthood, but eventually he did humbly return and ask his father's forgiveness, which was granted even before he arrived at the front gate of their property. He had to move closer to his father to experience the reality of his father's love. The earlier fracture of separation between the younger son and his father was fully restored.

The older brother was not at all disconnected from his father. He could not tolerate his father making a decision of which he did not approve. He expected his father to share his own judgmental opinions of his younger brother. It appears he had an unhealthy fusion with his father, reflecting his lack of respect for the decisions made by his father in this matter. He felt hurt because he had not been given his own party with his friends. It appears he was unhealthily connected and was likely enmeshed with his father. It seems that he was laboring to earn his father's love, in spite of his father's existing unconditional love. When the older brother refers to his brother as "this son of yours" and the fact that he boycotted the celebration of his brother's return indicates that he was probably disconnected from his brother Both sons were operating dysfunctionally toward their father, although at the opposite ends of the emotional spectrum.[10]

The seemingly healthy person in the family was the father. He treated his younger son as an adult, respecting his preference. He did not send private detectives to find him and force him to come home. He rejoiced that his wayward young son made the decision to eventually return to his family. When the older son rejected his invitation to celebrate, the father did not allow his older son's critical attitude to keep him from the celebration that he desired to provide. For this reason, the father does not appear enmeshed with his older son. He also treated his older son as an adult. He did not compel his older son to attend. He gave him freedom to choose. The father was the differentiated one in the family. Because of his differentiation, he could love both of his sons and was not dissuaded from organizing the celebration, where his great joy could be shared with their friends.

---

10. For additional discussion of this parable of Jesus see *Forgiveness: Unleashing a Transformational Process,* by Larry D. Ellis (Denver, CO: Adoration Publishing, 2010), 126-129.

We must not leave this important teaching of Jesus without addressing the context of this parable. This parable follows two other parables all taught to the religious leaders of the day. All three of them address how God, our Heavenly Father, has unconditional love for us and how he initiates with us based on his goodness, not ours. This relational boundary established by God provides an immeasurable level of grace toward us.

Nathan Courageously Confronts King David

In 2 Samuel 11 and 12, we read of the destructive behavior of David, the king of Israel. The story opens with king David watching a woman bathing from the top of his palace. Bathsheba was beautiful. She was married to Uriah the Hittite. David sent his messengers to bring her to him. David had sex with her, and she became pregnant with his child.

Uriah, Bathsheba's husband was a faithful soldier of king David. But because David wanted Bathsheba for himself, he needed everyone to assume the baby was Uriah's. If it became known that Bathsheba had been unfaithful to her husband, she would have been stoned. Because Uriah was too honorable, to follow the scheme of deception designed by David, David's solution was to kill him. Uriah's death made Bathsheba available to marry the king. David had the military commander place Uriah in a very dangerous position in the battle, where he would be killed. Uriah's wife grieved when she learned her husband had been killed in battle. When her mourning was over, which likely lasted no longer than a month, David brought her to the palace to become his wife.[11] She bore him a son. David's scheme had worked. But the Scriptures reported what David had done greatly displeased the Lord.[12]

At that point, the Lord sent the prophet Nathan to David. Nathan was likely a high-ranking court official of the powerful king

---

11. Robert D. Bergen, *1, 2 Samuel*, vol. 7, *The New American Commentary* (Nashville: Broadman & Holman Publishers, 1996), 368.
12. 2 Sam 11:27

David.¹³ He was a close, trusted advisor of David.¹⁴ Nathan told David a parable of two men who lived in a city. One was rich and one was poor. The rich man had many flocks and herds, but the poor man had only one little ewe lamb. The poor man loved his lamb. When the rich man received a guest in his home, he decided not to serve one of his own lambs, but instead took the poor man's only lamb and prepared a feast with it. Upon hearing this story, David expressed great anger against this rich man and said that man deserves to die, and he must restore the lamb fourfold. Nathan then boldly confronted the king and said,

> "You are the man!" Thus says the Lord, the God of Israel, "I anointed you king over Israel, and I delivered you out of the hand of Saul. And I gave you your master's house and your master's wives into your arms and gave you the house of Israel and of Judah.... Why have you despised the word of the Lord, to do what is evil in his sight? You have struck down Uriah the Hittite with the sword and have taken his wife to be your wife and have killed him with the sword of the Ammonites. Now therefore the sword shall never depart from your house, because you have despised me and have taken the wife of Uriah the Hittite to be your wife." (2 Sam 12:7-11)

This story, although it is historic, not a parable, also has two levels of meaning for us. One becomes clear as we reframe the context to one that is relevant today. The second level goes a bit deeper, probing our heart, calling us to change our values if necessary.

Nathan exhibited great courage before the king. Nathan was not intimidated by the king's power. Because Nathan saw the king as a separate person from himself, and because Nathan had a well-developed self, he could courageously confront the king describing

---

13. Jocelyn McWhirter, "Nathan the Prophet," *The Lexham Bible Dictionary,* ed. John D. Barry et al., (Bellingham, WA: Lexham Press, 2012, 2013, 2014, 2015).

14. 2 Sam 7, where Nathan provided important guidance to king David, for which the king was grateful to God.

the truth that both God and David knew about David's sinful behavior. He appears significantly differentiated from king David, because he had the boldness to confront David with his sins of adultery and murder, even though Nathan could have been put to death by the king's command. Nathan warned David because of the things he had done, he would suffer grave consequences by God's hand. As a result, David had a dramatic change of heart. He confessed saying, "I have sinned against the Lord." Nathan then said to David, "The Lord also has put away your sin; you shall not die" (2 Sam 12:12). Because Nathan had been faithful to courageously speak what God had led him to say, and because David confessed his destructive actions, God forgave him and did not impose the anticipated dire consequences. Had Nathan not had the courage and security he felt, because of his differentiation from the king, he might well have avoided his fearful confrontation that God had called him to undertake with the king. Nathan's boldness helped king David to confess and repent from his illicit behavior. Had he been enmeshed with David, he could have assumed whatever the king did was right. His story would then have been quite different. Fortunately, Nathan worshiped God, not the king.

Today we have few kings who we must serve and obey. We also have few legitimate prophets who speak directly from God. However, there is no shortage of men and women who covet things that belong to others and who are jealous of relationships that others have. The strong courage of speaking truth modeled by Nathan is to become a part of our lifestyle. The jealousy of David toward Uriah led David to bring about death to one of his faithful subjects. Perhaps another deeper lesson to learn here, in addition to Nathan's example of courage, good boundaries, and differentiation is for each of us to respect one another. Looking only at this event in David's life, he clearly violated at least half of the ten commandments delivered to Moses.[15] He did so with malice and forethought, taking what he wanted and

---

15. Exod 20.

secretly having one of his faithful, loyal soldiers murdered to gain moral acceptance by this deception. Even so, God was at work in his life through the brave, bold, and truthful Nathan, a man who was faithful to both God and king David. The ultimate end result of Nathan living an obedient and differentiated life with the king was David's repentance of his terrible actions and his restoration by God. May Nathan's life of courage as well as David's rapid move to confession become incorporated into our lives.

Other Prominent People with Strong Boundaries

Scripture records many historic followers of God who also had strong boundaries and who lived lives congruent with those boundaries. I will examine Moses, Job, Daniel, Shadrack, Meshach, Abednego, and a few others.

Moses

Moses led the Israelites out of bondage in Egypt and led them to the promised land. He loved and was obedient to God. Moses left his brother Aaron in charge of the Israelites while he went up on the mountain to receive guidance from God about how they were to live their lives. After receiving the ten commandments from God, God told him his people had become spiritually corrupt. Moses returned to his people and found under the direct guidance of Aaron they had fabricated a golden calf idol which they were now worshiping. Exodus records,

> And as soon as he came near the camp and saw the calf and the dancing, Moses' anger burned hot, and he threw the tablets out of his hands and broke them at the foot of the mountain. He took the calf that they had made and burned it with fire and ground it to powder and scattered it on the water and made the people of Israel drink it. (Ex 32:10-20)

Moses first confronted Aaron, whom he had placed in charge. Knowing that God planned to destroy them for their abandonment of God and worship of a golden calf idol, Moses returned to the mountain to intercede and hopefully appeal to God to spare their lives. We see a number of healthy boundaries lived out by Moses. He was faithful to God and was not hesitant to confront those who had abandoned God, including his own family. He was faithful to the Israelites, because he successfully interceded for their continued lives. He maintained integrity to what he knew he had been called to do in leading his people, despite their unfaithfulness to God. Moses could have been tempted to disconnect from his people or even God. God even offered to kill the Israelites and start a new nation with Moses, but Moses refused.

Moses was not enmeshed with either God, his brother Aaron, or the Israelites. He had a strong enough self to rebuke Aaron and his people. He also the confidence in God's love, because he appealed for mercy on his people's behalf. He also was connected to God, his brother, and his people as well, interceding and appealing to everyone. He had the proper balance between connectedness and individuality.

Job

In the book of Job. we learn that he was a good man who feared God and hated evil. He was wealthy and had a large close-knit family. He had a non-negotiable commitment to follow and worship God, no matter what happened. Through no fault of is own, he lost his wealth, servants, and children. His response recorded in the Scriptures was "Then Job arose and tore his robe and shaved his head and fell on the ground and worshiped. And he said, 'Naked I came from my mother's womb, and naked shall I return. The Lord gave, and the Lord has taken away; blessed be the name of the Lord'" (Job 1:20-21).[16]

Many people close to him urged him to blame and reject God for allowing these traumas in Job's life. Even his wife said, "Do you still hold fast your integrity? Curse God and die" (Job 2:9). His response to her was to accuse her of being a foolish woman and asking how could they have received all the good from God and then reject God based on their experience of what she considered evil. Job also had three friends, "Eliphaz the Temanite, Bildad the Shuhite and Zophar the Naamathite" who arrived and at first seemed to feel great empathy and sadness for Job's great losses.[17] However, with these kind of friends, one would not need any enemies. Each of them presented extensive declarations about him being punished for his own sins, entirely missing the reality of God's working with Job. Job repeatedly refuted their arguments. He maintained a strong personal faith never giving in to their perspective never turning away from God, no matter what happened to him and despite their words. Job maintained his boundary of trusting God despite external pressures from those close to him exhorting him to do otherwise. Continuing to place one's trust in God amidst extreme suffering that seems unfair in the moment is a lifestyle boundary that many people do not embrace. Job never abandoned his boundary to follow God. He was neither enmeshed nor disconnected from God or those around him. His actions and his declarations of his heart make that reality perfectly clear.

Daniel

Daniel was a young, handsome, and educated member of the royal Israelite family. Daniel was brought before king Nebuchadnezzar

---

16. Major Contributors and Editors, "Tearing of Clothes," *The Lexham Bible Dictionary*, ed. John D. Barry et al. (Bellingham, WA: Lexham Press, 2016). This was a way of mourning and sometimes an act of repentance; For the Israelites, shaving the head was also a sign of mourning.

17. Robert L. Alden, *Job*, vol. 11, *The New American Commentary* (Nashville: Broadman & Holman Publishers, 1993), 68.

of Judah to become a teacher of the language and literature of the Babylonians in the palace. The author of Daniel writes, "But Daniel resolved that he would not defile himself with the king's food, or with the wine that he drank" (Daniel 1:8). Daniel established a dietary boundary, quite in contrast to the other young men selected by the king. He would not eat the fancy non-Kosher foods and the wine that the king would provide. This would have been an insult to the king during this time, and those in charge of Daniel's care feared this choice was in defiance of the king. This decision resulted in him actually being healthier than those who indulged themselves with the rich foods and drink. In order to make them healthy also, the diet for other servants was then changed to eliminate the wine and fancy meats.[18] Daniel proved himself as a faithful servant of the king. But eventually a new king, Darius, issued an edict that anyone, except Darius himself, who prays to any god or man during the first thirty days of his reign, should be placed into the lions' den. This assured their death as punishment for disobeying the king. Daniel chose to defy this edict. He remained faithful to God, even if doing so should cost him his life. He maintained his boundary of continuing to pray to God. Daniel got down on his knees, gave thanks to the Hebrew God, and asked for his help. Because of the new king's edict, Daniel was quickly sentenced to the lions' den. God honored Daniel's prayer, because he was delivered unhurt the next day.[19] Once again, we learn that remaining faithful to honor God and renouncing activities that displease him, can come with the threat of being killed. Certainly, many middle eastern Christians live under that threat every day. Some lifestyle boundaries carry this price.

Shadrach, Meshach, and Abednego

Later in the book of Daniel, we learn king Nebuchadnezzar fabricated a ninety foot tall golden idol, and he commanded when

---

18. Dan 1.
19. Dan 6.

certain music was played all his subjects were to fall down and worship this golden image. When the king learned he had three Jewish leaders over Babylon who were not obeying him, he had them brought before him and confronted them promising he would have them burned, if they did not comply. He was furious by their insubordination to his authority. The book of Daniel records,

> Shadrach, Meshach, and Abednego answered and said to the king, "O Nebuchadnezzar, we have no need to answer you in this matter. If this be so, our God whom we serve is able to deliver us from the burning fiery furnace, and he will deliver us out of your hand, O king. But if not, be it known to you, O king, that we will not serve your gods or worship the golden image that you have set up." (Dan 3:16-18)

The three maintained their boundary worshiping only the Hebrew God. This was in direct opposition to the king's command to worship the large golden idol. Consequently, they were bound and tossed into an extremely hot furnace. Their punishment was not only for refusing to bow down before the idol; their worst crime was defying the direct command of the king. The fire was so hot that the servants who threw them into the furnace were themselves burned to death. Yet, Shadrach, Meshach, and Abednego emerged unsinged and unharmed to see the king. When they walked out of the furnace the king began to offer praise to the God of these three men.[20] Because of their faithful maintenance of this boundary of worshiping only the Hebrew God, the king and his kingdom began to worship the one true God of Israel along with these three men.

Additional People with Strong Boundaries

A review of history will reveal a long list of people who maintained strong boundaries and were not manipulated by other people's desires and expectations. In addition to many examples in

---

20. Dan 3.

the Scriptures of such leaders, we also can learn from people such as Polycarp and Iraneus, both of whom were among the influential ancient church fathers. We also see similar character in people such as Martin Luther, Abraham Lincoln, Martin Luther King, Rosa Parks, Mother Teresa, and Nelson Mandela. None of these persons were perfect, yet each one established a boundary in their life for which they became famous, standing against the destructive pressures by those who opposed them.

Living with Healthy Boundaries

While our formation of boundaries is important, there is no particular virtue in simply forming arbitrary boundaries. It is possible to inadvertently establish a bad boundary. For example, someone could find a particular job more difficult than they wish to tolerate. Should they quit their job, while having no replacement job and also become dependent upon others for their financial needs, they might have set a poor boundary for a good value of independence.

The establishment of good boundaries is the responsibility of all Christ-followers. There are some arenas where boundaries would be universal, but many need to be individually established. Healthy boundaries for each person can be unique. They can be based on character values. We are to follow the values that God has revealed to us. Some of these will include physical protection for ourselves and others. We should resist the temptation to compromise the uniqueness that God has created in us if such actions are motivated primarily to please others. Sometimes boundaries can simply be established to avert certain risks or dangers and can even be based on our personal preferences. These limits can involve the movies we see, the books we read, or the type of music we enjoy. When social justice is a boundary value for us, we must sometimes intervene where we see evil being acted out, even if doing so can be costly to us. We also need not fear coming to God asking him to intervene, so long as we have a humble heart toward God.

Our boundaries must be based on purposeful, good values we embrace. Rigid, inflexible boundaries can sometimes disconnect us from other people, should we become unresponsive to *their* needs and boundaries. When we develop clear boundaries that honor God and respect those around us and live consistently within them, we will reduce the likelihood of being manipulated or controlled by others. We also then become more visible to others, as we choose to disclose to them more and more of who we really are.

Wise risk-taking requires clear and defined boundaries. We will sometimes break outside our typical patterns of behavior and take some risks in relationships as Nathan did with king David, because we have clear and intentional boundaries. We may find we experience a deepening, unconditional love for others as the prodigal's dad did. When we have healthy boundaries, we will feel less responsible for other people's feelings and cease blaming others for our own mistakes. With healthy relational boundaries we will maintain a proper balance between independence from and connection with others. We will give more freedom to others and experience more freedom from others.

Insights from Scripture

The psychological terminology used in this book such as boundaries, enmeshment, disconnection, and differentiation, provide a clear classification of behavior, when evaluated in light of the Scripture passages presented here. Even though these categories are not explicitly listed in the Bible, they are implicitly presented through the character and behavior of the many biblical characters discussed.

To become differentiated requires that we develop good personal boundaries. We see good examples in Jesus, the prodigal's father, Nathan, Moses, Job, Daniel, Shadrach, Meshach, and Abednego. Each person lived their life out of intentional boundaries they had in place. We see enmeshed behavior in the prodigal's older brother and Aaron. They were living their lives out of what they believed others wanted them to do. Their enmeshment blinded their ability to see clearly from God's frame of reference for their lives and those persons around them. We also see the destructive disconnection that the prodigal had as he separated from his family. Perhaps the action of disconnection from a personal relationship is the saddest loss of all. As long as a person maintains the disconnection from someone, there is no possibility of a return to reconciliation and a loving relationship.

Finally, we see the dramatic shift toward differentiated behavior as a result of change in both David and the prodigal as they humble themselves. The change that is brought on in their lives gives us a glimmer of hope that even when the relationship seems forever fractured, it can be fully restored when the one pronouncing the sentence of disconnection is influenced to change their heart and behavior.

As we have seen, Jesus lived his life with intentional boundaries. He also gave us some examples of how we are to do the same thing. Jesus' parable about the loving father of two sons illustrates many examples of good boundaries. This father did not control either of his adult sons' decisions, even though he disagreed with some of their choices. He gave them freedom to make wrong choices. He did not issue judgments against either of his sons. He did not allow his older son's judgments against him or his brother rob him of the joyous celebration of the return of his wayward son.

Even though the powerful king David could have ordered to have Nathan killed, just as he had orchestrated Uriah's death, Nathan had the unwavering courage to confront the king about his immoral behavior. This was made possible in part because of Nathan's secure sense of himself and his God. Because of Nathan's clear commitment to honor God, king David was drawn back to God. Nathan was not enmeshed with the king; Nathan was differentiated from king David.

Looking at these Scriptures make it clear that dysfunctional behavior as well as emotionally healthy and differentiated behavior are not new innovations, but have been seen in humanity for thousands of years. These dysfunctions are still thriving in our culture today. Prominent people in politics, business, and religious leadership often seem unable "to remember" events from their own lives, while condemning others for doing the very things they have done. The boundaries they reveal in these circumstances are no longer admirable boundaries. They become entirely self-serving at least for the moment.

We can learn from careful observation of mature adult relationships where people are differentiated. We can develop the discernment to recognize this behavior in ourselves and in others. This is the first step toward our learning how to protect ourselves from being abused by others and allowing ourselves to exhibit destructive behavior toward those around us. Another thing we observe from the Scriptures is that maintaining strong boundaries can be risky for us. Maintaining certain boundaries can be costly, but doing so can also be incredibly rewarding.

We need not be limited by our bashfulness and fears about changing. As we depart relational adolescence to mature spiritually and emotionally and learn to operate with intentional, healthy boundaries, we can experience a transformed lifestyle of adult emotional behavior. We need not be bound by our past experiences, our woundedness, or our self-centered behavior.

Chapter 7

The Distortion of Authority

The Foundation of Authority

Healthy relationships must operate with a healthy understanding of authority. In this book, I provide a narrow examination of this subject, one that will be helpful, but certainly not exhaustive. Many people seek to manage other peoples' lives for them. The motives for these agendas can be quite varied. Understanding the basis of authority will greatly help the reader filter out the voices that are self-serving and not truly authoritative. The better we recognize these unhelpful voices, the wiser our decision-making will become.

In our western culture, there is a widespread rejection of many of the traditional, powerful, pervasive voices of authority. What has risen to the top is authority which primarily exists within ourselves. In some cases, we defer to the preferences of a democratic majority, to whom we partially entrust authority, as long as we agree with that particular majority. Should we disagree with that majority, we might consider ourselves not to be subject to that authority. In western cultures, we have become the arbiters of truth—our truth. Adding to that perspective, many people reject the idea of objective truth. We now allow each person to have their "own truth," which might well be completely at odds with other "truths."

Both the American political and religious cultures are filled with countless examples of these "conflicting truths." For example, American political conservatives believe liberty grows as we reduce the power of the government. Many people believe economic growth is stifled by the government from over-taxation and excessive regulation. This is their "truth." The political liberal frames economic "truth" quite differently. He believes economic growth is stimulated by powerful government programs and regulations, because these programs, justly administered, present the needed growth opportunity for people that the private capitalistic sector is not motivated to provide. These two very different "truths" address the same issue of desired economic growth.

In the Christian community, a strong Calvinist believes God causes human suffering so the glory of God will be revealed. But many other Christians believe when suffering surfaces, God's agenda is to bring redemption out of suffering caused by flawed persons, bad choices, and arbitrary disasters. Many believers feel that God will not rob us of free will, which can result in suffering as well. Others maintain the purpose of suffering is to bring everyone closer to God. The cause of human suffering does not seem uniformly clear. How we frame our view of truth dramatically impacts how we choose to live our live and the roles we carry out with one another.

People are often firm in their conviction of these conflicted perspectives and sometimes close their minds and hearts, completely refusing to accept the position and persons who do not agree with them. Such myopic, dualistic thinking brings about destruction of any sense of community and undermines a willingness to learn and grow together. If after constructive conversation we still disagree, at least we have had the opportunity to learn how and why the other person holds their perspective. These diversities of understandings are all around us, especially in this day of independent thinking and individualized assessment of truth. God calls us to hold fast to the central non-compromised revealed truths he has clearly provided and exhibit grace toward others on all the rest. We are to carefully discern what issues are so significant that they must divide us.

The use and abuse of authority has been embedded in human relationships ever since the dawn of humanity. Soon after God created them, both Adam and Eve looked to the wrong authorities for their decision-making. They were tempted by external forces and ultimately turned inward to themselves for "authority" to override the clear guidance given to them by God.[1] When they made these choices, they did not take personal responsibility for their decisions, but instead both persons blamed someone else for the choices that they made. Those choices not only had devastating consequences for them, but continued to impact all of humanity that followed. Defying God's authority is never a smart move for anyone. Christians have always claimed to recognize and operate under the authority of God, revealed in Jesus. We are called to become good stewards of all of God's creation. Remember, a good steward is one who is taking responsible care of something that actually belongs to someone else. Each of us is accountable to God for our own lives.

While diversity in theology and great liberty is found within Christianity, there are a few non-negotiable boundaries of authority we must embrace to become a faithful Christ-follower. Christians believe ultimate authority is not found in governments, group collectives, or individuals, but belongs to God. Theologian and author Walter Woods summarizes the Christian message when he writes,

> Rather than accept God's dominion in their lives, human beings have chosen to live in ways that declare their independence from God and his life-giving purpose. This causes alienation from God and accounts for the evil and hostility found in human life (Gen. 3). These effects lead to new rejections of God in an ongoing process that enmeshes all people (Rom. 3:9; 5:12). The term sin can refer to the cause, state, or results of this complex condition of evil and alienation.
>
> Given this state of affairs, reconciliation necessarily requires the overcoming of sin by means of repentance and forgiveness and ultimately by an inner transformation that eliminates the tendency to sin and alienation (Jer. 31:33; Ezek. 36:25–28; Ps. 51:10). This could be

---

1. Gen 2.

accomplished only by God's special intervention, which took place through the incarnation of Jesus Christ. Because he was fully divine and fully human, Jesus was uniquely able to mediate between and draw together God and the human family. By his suffering, death, and resurrection, Jesus reconciled us to God and made possible the forgiveness of our sins and the hope of a human life marked by justice, peace, and unity (Rom. 5:1–11; Col. 1:19–22; 2 Cor. 5:18–19).[2]

The Bible is clear about God's authority, yet Christians frequently neglect to emphasize this truth. For example, Jesus said to his disciples, "All authority in heaven and on earth has been given to me. Go therefore and make disciples of all nations, baptizing them in the name of the Father and of the Son and of the Holy Spirit, teaching them to observe all that I have commanded you. And behold, I am with you always, to the end of the age" (Matt 28:18-20). This teaching known as the Great Commission is not commonly used to convey the truth that Jesus has all authority at all levels over all things. Instead, many readers of Scripture co-opt the passage to promote primarily the last portion of this passage overlooking the first portion. Both parts of this message by Jesus are important. In the most reliable Greek manuscripts the only commanding verb is to *make* disciples. In Greek, however, the participles of going, baptizing, and teaching others to live out all Jesus had commanded imply the same imperative by expanding upon what would be the process of making disciples. But all of this is done under Jesus' authority, not ours. Jesus' backdrop for the mission of this verse leaves no doubt that he is the one with all authority throughout this entire process. He does not relinquish his authority to any human agent or organization.

Woods' brief summary of the Christian narrative explains the authoritative message and process that Jesus provides. A connected

---

2. Walter J. Woods, "Reconciliation and Priesthood," in *The Complete Library of Christian Worship*, vol. 1, *The Biblical Foundations of Christian Worship*, ed. Robert E. Webber (Nashville, TN: Star Song Pub. Group, 1993), 347.

relationship to God is founded upon what he has done and by our acceptance of Jesus to connect us with his Father. Jesus' life of love and servanthood is a template from God which shows us how we are to love one another. His lifestyle is rooted in the practice of unconditional forgiveness of one another and the absence of retaliation for offenses committed against us.[3] These two Christian values are in direct opposition to much of today's western culture. Learning to love others in the ways that God does will fundamentally shift our relationships toward being based on love and respect not power or manipulation. When that basis is established, our relationships will become differentiated, not enmeshed or cut off, because we are embracing the image of God he has bestowed upon each of us.

Hearing God

The natural consequence of our embracing the truth that authority comes from God is that we can then confidently listen to what he teaches us. We become the recipients of his wisdom. When we think of hearing God, I do not mean that we hear an aural sound of his voice speaking in our native language giving us step-by-step guidance on everything we face in life. Nonetheless, Scripture presents us with a number of ways to discern God's leading in our lives. We will examine several of these ways.

The starting point for hearing anyone is to slow down our busy lives and listen. The psalmist writes, "Be still, and know that I am God" (Ps 46:10a). The Gospel of John records these words of Jesus, "My sheep hear my voice, and I know them, and they follow me" (John 10:27). The psalmist prays to God, "I have stored up your word in my heart, that I might not sin against you" (Ps 119:10). The author of Proverbs writes, "Your word is a lamp to my feet and a light to my path" (Ps 119:105). These references to the word refer to the Scriptures that they had at that time, the books of the Law (the

---

3. Larry D. Ellis, *Forgiveness: Unleashing a Transformational Process* (Denver, CO: Adoration Publishing Company, 2010).

Torah).[4] He also wrote, "Where there is no guidance, a people falls, but in an abundance of counselors there is safety" (Prov 11:14). Not only do we have the great benefit of the Scriptures, but we also have keen insight from those who can give us wise counsel. Studying the Scriptures and listening to the community of God should be the bedrock of our discernment process for God's guidance.

Centuries later, Paul wrote, "Do not be conformed to this world, but be transformed by the renewal of your mind, that by testing you may discern what is the will of God, what is good and acceptable and perfect" (Rom 12:2). Careful listening to God requires a change in our frame of reference from us being in the center of our lives to us recognizing God in the center of our lives. This shift is the foundation of our transformed mind.

When we are seeking to hear God through the Scriptures, know there is always a cultural setting for every Scripture. There are issues known to the original hearers that might not be known to us today. We are often tempted to insert our own cultural perspectives where the Scriptures are silent. As sincere people read Scripture, they frequently view it through their own worldview and often appropriate the Scripture as today's guidance. Something that was correct, wise guidance in certain cultures at a particular point in time might not be appropriate in a different context or time. For example, the Old Testament gives explicit details for worship at the Tabernacle and the Temple, including exact building construction specifications, décor, and furnishings. The Jews also prescribed many Jewish regulations of behavior that when faithfully observed were considered the hallmark of pleasing God in that period. Those ancient mandates to the Israelites and regulations by the Jews have never been considered mandates in Christian worshiping communities.

In order to learn the important, underlying truths in Scriptures, it is important to know who is speaking, who is being addressed, why they were being instructed, and whether the scriptural instruction

---

4. The books of Law were Genesis, Exodus, Leviticus, Numbers, and Deuteronomy.

has particular relevance only to a certain culture or is of a universal nature. Even worse is the all-to-common practice of lifting a verse out of its original context and then viewing it as a personal statement to us individually. This process will create a fundamental misunderstanding of what the Scripture is teaching. For example, a well known passage from Jeremiah states, "For I know the plans I have for you, declares the Lord, plans for welfare and not for evil, to give you a future and a hope. Then you will call upon me and come and pray to me, and I will hear you. You will seek me and find me, when you seek me with all your heart" (Jer 29:11-13). This has been imprinted upon many graduation presents, providing a "blessing" for people facing unknown changes in their future. "The message is clear: don't worry; God loves you and has a wonderful plan for your life."[5] But, this verse is not about anyone's career plans. It most definitely was not addressed to people today. It was a specific encouragement that God extended to the Jews that were in exile in Babylon. Although the time had not arrived for their freedom, God was reminding them at the end of the seventy year exile, he would keep his promise and return them to the promised land. Any attempts to use this text to teach something supplemental to this truth is likely misusing this important promise of God.

Even though the study of Scripture is critical, not all the guidance we seek from God will be found in the Scripture. Scripture will not reveal to us which of two houses we are to purchase, what college to attend, or even whom we should marry. Scripture will not answer the question of why one seemingly innocent person suffers while another person does not. But Scripture will give us God's revelation for guidance and God's values out of which we can live.

Fortunately, God provides an additional, cherished layer of communication with us. John advises us that Jesus promised to give

---

5. E. Randolph Richards and Brandon J. O'Brien, *Misreading Scripture with Western Eyes: Removing Cultural Blinders to Better Understand the Bible* (Downers Grove, IL: InterVarsity Press, 2012), 192.

his advocate, the Holy Spirit, to his disciples and us.[6] The mission of the Holy Spirit is to lead us. Jesus also clearly states that the consequence of our loving him is our following of his commandments.

> If you love me, obey my commandments. And I will ask the Father, and he will give you another Advocate, who will never leave you. He is the Holy Spirit, who leads into all truth. The world cannot receive him, because it isn't looking for him and doesn't recognize him. But you know him, because he lives with you now and later will be in you. (John 14:15-17)

The Holy Spirit is not our advocate. He is God's advocate. His agenda is to reveal and persuade us of God's intention and desires. At times, his Spirit speaks direct guidance to our heart for which we will be accountable to God. This experience was not the norm in the Old and New Testament records. But, through the Holy Spirit credible contemporary Christian disciples report a number of such experiences. If you are not familiar with this portion of history, check out the ministry of John Wimber of the Vineyard Ministries and many Christians who have discerned that God has faithfully answered their prayers.

Our discernment about hearing God goes beyond operating with a hunch or even our own intuition. Wise discernment of God's leading of us comes to us through a spiritually transformed mind, not just our cognitive intellect. Though the Scriptures are a primary guide, our interpretations and applications are not infallible. When we are discerning God's wisdom for us in a particular decision, it is much more common for us to act out of a sense of internal peace, trusting God to continually unfold his will as we move forward striving to live out of values God has revealed to us though the Scriptures and confirmed by a reliable, authentic Christian community.

We have this word of encouragement from the Psalms, "Delight yourself in the Lord and he will give you the desires of your heart" (Ps

---

6. In Romans chapter 8, the apostle Paul writes that everyone who is in Christ has the Holy Spirit within them.

37:4). If we delight ourselves in and follow God, he promises to provide us with desires that please him as he also fulfills these desires. But we have a warning given to the prophet Jeremiah, "The heart is deceitful above all things, and desperately sick; who can understand it" (Jer 17:9). There is no cookbook formula to unconditionally know what God is speaking to us. We must always acknowledge a level of mystery accompanied by faith in his leading of us. Then we decide and take actions based on our discernments. Our trust is always in God's faithfulness and his love for us, not our own skill in finding out God's will.

Authority over Other Persons' Lives

Since early recorded history, authority has almost always been hierarchical. Gods were on top. Under the gods were the rulers, who acted on behalf of the gods, followed by others with lesser authority, who acted on behalf of the rulers. Sometimes the Pharaohs in Egypt and the Caesars in Rome were considered gods by themselves and their subjects. There were various descending seats of authority down to the common folk who were expected to do precisely as they were told on all matters by those above them. These common persons had no authority within society. Personal relationships that crossed these classes of people were almost non-existent. Almost everyone had people in authority over them.

Hierarchical authority is also experienced by anyone who has been in a military organization. Various levels of officers hold the command positions in all branches of the military. Much of the corporate world operates in the same manner with directors hiring CEOs who lead the managers who lead the employees. In most developed countries, the police, along with many government agencies, claim authority over much of what we do or want to do. Respect for those with morally sound authority can bring a level of order to a chaotic society. But, when one or more of these important elements—legitimate authorization or moral and just actions—is absent from leadership, anarchy can result.

Some Christians have believed they have been given Jesus' authority over the earth, and people in particular. This is a complete delusion. Christians do not have God's authority. God retains it, exclusively. Very few subjects promoted by Christian teachers have caused more pain and abuse in relationships than destructive teaching about authority. A hierarchical structure for a community, church, and family is efficient, but it is not likely to nurture growth and independent thinking and practices. Some churches teach oppressive values today, although such thinking is not a twenty-first-century innovation. This thinking has been around for centuries and has been normally associated with a hierarchical worldview.[7] Independent thinking within these Christian communities can be classified as "unorthodox," rebellious, apostasy, or heresy, and this labeling quickly becomes abusive.

Emotional and spiritual maturity implies people take full responsibility before God and others for the decisions they make. In contrast, taking responsibility to manage another adult's personal life is often controlling and likely self-serving behavior. This is true even if the authority figure genuinely believes they are doing God's work of shepherding within a Christian community. When people are "instructed" to live their lives under the tutelage of someone, and then confronted and disciplined for a failure of not conforming to the prescribed behavior, the basis for adult Christianity is eroded. A red flag should go up anytime people are not free to make personal decisions contrary to the opinions of church leaders.

Power and authority are not the same thing, though they are sometimes used interchangeably. Power is the ability to pressure and compel someone to do something they otherwise might not choose to do. Anyone holding a loaded gun and pointing it at us, will probably motivate us to do what they want. They have the power. However,

---

7. Larry D. Ellis, "Role of Christian Women," accessed July 7, 2016, http://www.worshipandchurchmusic.com/role_of_christian_women.htm.

authority means one has the moral or legal right and responsibility to exercise power. A judge has the legal authority to pronounce us not guilty in the eyes of the law or guilty and send us to prison. One who has a higher rank than someone else in the military has authority over the lower-ranking person. Some people would argue certain Christian leaders have authority over other Christians' lives. I would argue that such teaching is not found in the Scriptures, and trying to impose that structure is in direct conflict with the instructions of Jesus and the apostles. To illustrate the point, we can examine a few passages of Scripture.

Several Scripture passages are often used to promote the use of power and authority in the church and sometimes even over our personal decisions that do not relate to the church. In one text, Paul describes an important element about relationships writing to the Christ-followers in Galatia. He writes,

> Brothers, if anyone is caught in any transgression, you who are spiritual should restore him in a spirit of gentleness. Keep watch on yourself, lest you too be tempted. Bear one another's burdens, and so fulfill the law of Christ. For if anyone thinks he is something, when he is nothing, he deceives himself. But let each one test his own work, and then his reason to boast will be in himself alone and not in his neighbor. For each will have to bear his own load (Gal 6:1-5).

This passage is sometimes morphed into the following distorted teaching: when you see a brother who is in sin, doing something he should not be doing, or neglecting something that should be a priority, Christian brothers are responsible to get him straightened out and return his behavior to what is deemed proper by the truly spiritual brothers. In practice, being gentle is not always emphasized, because the far more important mission is the behavioral change of the wayward brother. The wayward person is exhorted and then given a quotation from the letter to the Hebrews, "Obey your leaders and submit to them, for they are keeping watch over your souls, as those who will have to give an account" (Heb 13:17). In such circumstances, submission is usually understood as an explicit command from God to do what the spiritual leader says to do.

In this understanding of the Bible, if the wayward person does not straighten out as directed, then the wayward brother and perhaps even the leader will be punished by God. Somehow, the prospect of dire consequences for them or their leaders is to motivate the wayward one to reform. If the wayward person refuses to suitably amend their behavior, the brother is to sever his relationship with that person. Only when submission has caused the required change in behavior can the relationship be restored. This authoritarian model for the family and the church is not at all what Paul is promoting. This passage will be discussed below.

In Galatians 6, Paul is not calling believers to take action to reprimand a believer who has willingly committed a sin. Paul is specifically writing about Christians who are caught like an animal captured in a trap or one who is "in over their head." Other translators of the New Testament use the word overcome.[8] This condition might be when there is an ongoing disregard or ignorance of what Jesus expects of his followers. While we might observe someone living outside what we believe as proper behavior for a Christian, and perhaps even share our perception with him or her, we are not responsible *for* anyone's spirituality except our own. We are not to assume the role of spiritual and moral management for our Christian brothers and sisters. Instead, Galatians clearly teaches we are responsible *to* them, being faithful, encouraging, supportive, and at times even confrontive. Theologian Gerald Borchert explains that this concern need not relate only to sin,

> ...but could include many other matters, such as illness, loss of loved ones, problems of oppression, persecution, hunger, family and work issues, and many others. Paul exhorts the spiritual person to be a burden-bearer, one

---

8. Gal 6:1, the New Living Translation (NLT) and the Revised Standard Version (RSV).

who exhibits the overarching characteristic of love, as well as other virtues.[9]

After Paul exhorted the Christians in Galatia about living a life of deference and not passing judgments upon those Christians who see some things differently from themselves, he reminds them we will all stand individually before God. He stated, "So then each of us will give an account of himself to God" (Rom 14:12). No doubt, this personal reporting to God will keep most of us sufficiently busy.

We do not report on other people's actions. Nor are we accountable to God for them or their actions. That abusive, authoritarian management of other's lives is precisely what was happening in the church at Galatia, and Paul was insisting they cease their judging and prideful confrontations of others . So in fact, Paul is actually teaching the exact opposite of what many believe. Paul is not establishing a program of judging and punishment for their members. He is establishing a process of discernment, confirmation, and discipline for those who are committing the most egregious sins. Paul is not promoting uber tolerance, because he places specific boundaries and conditions on how we are to approach, care for, and serve one another. He is describing the nature of help and encouragement that should be experienced individually by those within our faith community.

The second century pastor Clement of Alexandria makes a clear distinction that Christians are called to support one another when there is a great need. This support can take the form of disclosure of our perceptions, but he makes no implication of control of other believers. He wrote,

> For as the mirror is not evil to an ugly man because it shows him what he is like; and as the physician is not evil to the sick man because he tells him of his fever,—for the physician is not the cause of the fever, but only points out

---

9. Gerald L. Borchert, *Galatians: Tyndale Cornerstone Biblical Commentary*, vol. 14, (Carol Stream, IL: Tyndale House Publishers, Inc., 2007), 329.

the fever;—so neither is He, that reproves, ill-disposed towards him who is diseased in soul.[10]

The desired end of any such encouragement, disclosure, or confrontation is always to be the restoration of the sister or brother to a life of renewed and strengthened relationship with God

The theology of policing one another is not at all new. The ancient church father Bishop of Constantinople (c. 373-c. 381), St. John Chrysostom, teaching on Galatians 6, spoke against the perversion of authority in his own day, emphasizing this role of coming alongside of one is not for when they have committed a sin, but when they are overtaken. He taught that we are to approach them in a spirit of meekness, without judgment. We are to do this with the greatest of humility, so we are not overtaken with temptation ourselves. None of us have reached perfection. Some challenges are simply too much to endure alone. We need the encouragement and support from other Christ-followers.

In his commentary on this passage from Galatians Chrysostom wrote,

> "Brethren, even if a man be overtaken in any trespass." Forasmuch as under cover of a rebuke they gratified their private feelings, and professing to do so for faults which had been committed, were advancing their own ambition, he says, "brethren, if a man be overtaken." He said not if a man commit but if he be "overtaken" that is, if he be carried away.[11]

---

10. Clement of Alexandria, "The Instructor," in *Fathers of the Second Century: Hermas, Tatian, Athenagoras, Theophilus, and Clement of Alexandria (Entire)*, ed. Alexander Roberts, James Donaldson, and A. Cleveland Coxe, vol. 2, The Ante-Nicene Fathers (Buffalo, NY: Christian Literature Company, 1885), 231.

11. John Chrysostom, "Commentary of St. John Chrysostom, Archbishop of Constantinople, on the Epistle of St. Paul the Apostle to the Galatians," in *Saint Chrysostom: Homilies on Galatians, Ephesians, Philippians, Colossians, Thessalonians, Timothy, Titus, and Philemon*, ed. Philip Schaff, trans. Gross Alexander with Anonymous, vol. 13, A Select Library of the Nicene and Post-Nicene Fathers of the Christian Church, First Series (New York: Christian Literature Company, 1889), 43–44.

The bishop teaches those who are spiritual to restore the person. He does not say to "chastise" or "judge" such a person, but to "restores such a one" in a spirit of meekness. Paul does not write "in meekness," rather in a spirit of meekness, implying that to be able to administer correction with mildness is a spiritual gift. In order that we not exalt ourselves, we are also to examine ourselves so we are not tempted.[12] Chrysostom then teaches we are to bear one another's burdens. He wrote,

> It being impossible for man to be without failings, he exhorts them not to scrutinize severely the offences of others, but even to bear their failings, that their own may in turn be borne by others. As, in the building of a house, all the stones hold not the same position, but one is fitted for a corner but not for the foundations, another for the foundations, and not for the corner, so too is it in the body of the Church. The same thing holds in the frame of our own flesh; notwithstanding which, the one member bears with the other, and we do not require every thing from each, but what each contributes in common constitutes both the body and the building.[13]

The bishop continues, as this lifestyle is lived out, the law of Christ is complete, making all of us in common. He cites the example of a man being cantankerous or angry and we are dull-tempered or boring and lacking liveliness, we should endure his forceful emotions and he our sluggishness. Because of both our forbearance we can not take offense with each other's shortcomings and complete what is lacking in each other. It is like the case of the body, if every part had to do everything, it could never exist. He concludes his teaching on this passage exhorting them to examine themselves and their own work and remain humble.

Here he shows that we ought to be scrutinizers of our lives, and this not lightly, but carefully to weigh our actions; as for example,

---

12. Ibid.
13. Ibid.

"...if thou hast performed a good deed, consider whether it was not from vain glory, or through necessity, or malevolence, or with hypocrisy, or from some other human motive."[14]

Chrysostom is clearly explaining there were those who were rebuking other Christians for what they perceived as sinful actions. That practice of rebuking was explicitly not Paul's instruction from the Galatians passage. The observation we make which causes us to reach out should be when someone is overtaken or has stepped beyond their ability to stand firm in following God. The action we are to take has one purpose, to come alongside and bear their burden with them in a spirit of meekness and servanthood. We are to extend forbearance toward one another and lend a hand when they need help. Our conversation with them cannot contain judgments of their actions, because should we have judgments, we, too, will be tempted to live apart from how God intends.

Because we cannot expect complete spiritual maturity in everyone around us, we are compelled to be gracious, forgiving, and helpful to others, just as they are to extend the same graciousness, forgiveness, and helpfulness toward us when we fail. Christians are to notice when someone is overcome with actions or circumstances over which they are unable to get relief without help. In these circumstances, we are exhorted to come alongside them and take some of the load upon ourselves, until such time as they can successfully manage without our direct help.

The servant imagery Chrysostom employs is in contrast to the authority-driven supervisory and management approach. Different stones in a building have different purposes. No one stone can support the entire load alone. Many traumas and temptations are far too heavy for any one of us to process alone. Since we are all flawed persons, we need one another to help make up for our own deficiencies. We are to work together to support each other. Paul informs us living this way completes the law of Christ. Theologian Gerald

---

14. Ibid.

Borchert writes, "Whatever 'the law of Christ' means, it is not a reference to law as the Judaizers viewed it.[15] For Paul, that was bondage. It meant either the *Torah*, the will of God as affirmed by Jesus, or perspectives and principles that Paul perceived as inherent in the gospel message."[16] Additionally, each of us is to authentically scrutinize our own lives. When we do a good deed, we must not do it for the personal glory and praise. Instead, we are to do it in grateful appreciation to God for his many blessings given to us. This, too, is a caution for us to live in humility rather than dominance or self-contentedness. The focus of Paul's message here is healthy and restored relationships. It is about being with one another in spite of our shortcomings, because we acknowledge our own short comings and heed that forbearance as well.

A brief passage alluded to earlier that might be seen as in opposition to this perspective is Hebrews 13:16-18. The author writes, "Do not neglect to do good and to share what you have, for such sacrifices are pleasing to God. Obey your leaders and submit to them, for they are keeping watch over your souls, as those who will have to give an account. Let them do this with joy and not with groaning, for that would be of no advantage to you" (Heb 12:16-17). A cursory reading might assume this passage commands all believers to blindly and consistently submit to the leaders in charge of a Christian community.

A reasonable study of this passage does lead one who is a part of a Christian community to recognize the spiritual responsibility for people to lead and guide the community to follow God. Clearly, blind submission would never be an option. The discernment of God's leading is never determined by a majority vote of teachers, elders, or deacons. In the passage above, the writer of Hebrews is exhorting them to follow their current leaders. He does not charge all Christians to follow all spiritual leaders in all situations. He is

---

15. Judaizers were early Christians who believed a good Christian must first become a good Jew.

16. Borchert, *Galatians*, 329.

also addressing the church (not individuals) to follow their collective leadership—not the prophetic word given by an individual person.

There is a superior, alternative explanation—we are to follow the leadership because at that time the New Testament had not yet been written or circulated. The leaders were simply telling them to live in the same manner that Jesus taught. The point was they were to obey Jesus, following his instructions. The Hebrew Christians were not exhorted to live their lives deferring all their decisions to the present spiritual leaders and await divine guidance and proclamations through their appointed leaders.

If unilateral submission had been the intention, the many Scriptures challenging us to learn and grow up spiritually would not have been provided. Writing about the Hebrew Scriptures, the psalmist wrote, "Your word is a lamp to my feet and a light to my path" and "How can a young man keep his way pure? By living according to your word" (Ps 119:105). Paul wrote to the Christ-followers in Corinth, "Brothers, do not be children in your thinking. Be infants in evil, but in your thinking be mature" (1 Cor 14:20). Paul also wrote the following to all the Christ-followers in Colossae, not the leaders of the church. "We have not ceased to pray for you, asking that you may be filled with the knowledge of his will in all spiritual wisdom and understanding, so as to walk in a manner worthy of the Lord, fully pleasing to him: bearing fruit in every good work and increasing in the knowledge of God" (Col 1:9-10). Here the writer is stating as they grow and live with spiritual wisdom, they will please the Lord.

Another Scripture passage that is often used to justify the use of managerial authority and power in the church is Matthew 18. This text is placed after Jesus' disciples asked who is the greatest in the Kingdom of Heaven and the importance of resisting temptations. It comes just before he teaches a parable to his disciples about the dire consequences of being unforgiving of others. It is within the context of ongoing humility and our liberal practicing of forgiveness that he presents this teaching. This teaching is completely consistent with

Paul's letter of instructions to the Colossians. In Matthew 18 he provided guidance on handling personal conflicts between those within the community of faith.

> If your brother sins against you, go and tell him his fault, between you and him alone. If he listens to you, you have gained your brother. But if he does not listen, take one or two others along with you, that every charge may be established by the evidence of two or three witnesses. If he refuses to listen to them, tell it to the church. And if he refuses to listen even to the church, let him be to you as a Gentile and tax collector. (Matt 18: 15-17)

The situation to which this text speaks is when our brother sins against us personally. Every use of the word "you" in this passage is singular. It is about the process for dealing with personal conflicts between individual Christians. This passage does not address either the church leadership or a congregation to attempt to compel an individual or a part of the church community to go along with the majority position on a matter. It does not apply to conflicts with those who are not part of the Christian community, and is not relevant to the reputation of the community with outsiders.

The text instructs anyone who has been offended to approach the one who has inflicted the pain and seek to restore a relationship of brotherly love. If there is no reconciliation we are to bring one or two other people along with us to verify the facts and be certain that any confrontation is done in a spirit of meekness. The desired end result is always to persuade that person to seek a restored relationship. If he or she continues to resist, we are to tell some of the details to the church with the goal of restoring the personal relationship. This ultimate step of intervention is no longer practiced in the vast majority of churches in the western world. In the days of the ancient church, such public humiliation might have more easily facilitated repentance leading to reconciliation. Today, in our consumer-driven Christian communities, such action might possibly ensure that the accused person would permanently withdraw from the church as if nothing has happened. The person might select a different church that would be unaware or perhaps more tolerant of their actions. If the person leaves, the desired agenda of relational healing would not happen. In fact, in many relationships the first two steps listed in the process of reconciliation are also avoided. Rather than directly confront someone who has hurt us, many people flee such a confrontive experience out of fear. Such people often enjoy gossiping with other people, and seek to align these other people with themselves, wanting to validate their judgments against the other person. Again, this ill-directed behavior is precisely what Paul is warning the Galatian Christians against. Neither should this be our practice today.

Finally, should this process be carried out but fail to bring about a redemptive change in the person's behavior , we are to treat the one who has wounded us as Jesus says we would treat a tax collector and Gentile. We can read how Jesus treated Zacchaeus the tax collector.[17] Jesus invited himself to Zacchaeus' home for dinner. Jesus invited Matthew, a tax collector, to follow him and become an apostle.[18] The religious leaders of the day accused Jesus of being a friend of tax collectors.[19] This allegation was made to discredit Jesus, but it was true. One can infer that we should treat them as one who is not a Christian, and therefore, withdraw the level of intimacy that we enjoy within the Christian community. We still must remain loving in hopes they will be drawn close to the heart of God, just as we would desire for all people. The goal can never be retaliation or shaming of the other person. In the context of a church community today, this might mean the offending person cannot assist in leading public worship or teaching within the church community. It cannot mean to shun them, because as Paul teaches in Galatians we are to have a spirit of meekness and gentleness toward them.

Even with all our gentleness and humility toward those within our sphere of influence, there are clearly certain types of behavior that

---

17. Luke 19:1-10.
18. Matt 9:9-13.
19. Matt 11:19.

cannot be tolerated within the Christian community. There are times where consequences of actions cannot be erased. In such dire situations, we must intervene at whatever level is needed to bring about cessation of victimization and bring about healing to the extent possible. Destructive behaviors cannot be sanctioned or ignored within the Christian community, especially if they are inflicting problems upon others who are being victimized by the behavior. This intervention might have even included when someone was promoting false teaching within the church. But, historically, this action primarily involved egregious sin. In 1 Corinthians 5 we read that some sins were so immoral that he urged them to turn a man over to Satan and completely avoid contact with them. The purpose of this isolation from the Christian community was so that his spirit might be saved by his repentance from these sins.

Paul does provide a short list of what he considered egregious sins necessitating a withdrawal of fellowship: sexual immorality, greed, being an idolater, reviler, drunkard, or swindler. It might be a move of grace to us by God that there is no exhaustive list in Scripture for those shortcomings that would require spiritual people to intervene with one who has walked away from God's heart. There is often no Scriptural guidance on precisely what matters require this level of intervention. We must make that discernment with great hesitation and humility. The thrust of the passage in Galatians gives the attitude that we are to have with those who we see are stumbling. It is the work of the Holy Spirit to convince others that what they are doing is wrong. We are to confront them with the truth about their actions. The passage is not the mandate to police others, at most only to share what we perceive with them, trusting that God will move them to repentance in order to be restored to full fellowship within the community. Many books have discuss in much more detail the responsibility to intervene when Christians are practicing destructive behavior. This small portion of this book simply presents the essence of these teachings. Should you decide to undertake a mission as this, do so only with the greatest humility, prayer, and courage.

It will come as a surprise to many people that the initiative for reconciliation is not to come only from those who have committed an offense, but anyone simply upon learning someone believes we have committed an offense against them. In Jesus' Sermon on the Mount, he said, "So if you are offering your gift at the altar and there remember that your brother has something against you, leave your gift there before the altar and go. First be reconciled to your brother, and then come and offer your gift" (Matt 5:23-24). All Christ-followers are called to initiate reconciliation with those from whom we are estranged. This applies to the victim, the perpetrator, and anyone who learns they are justly or even unjustly accused. In the New Testament we find no escape clause for anyone from this call to initiate reconciliation. We must all do it in every situation.

From each of these passages, we have calls to action. But, we are given no authority to force anyone to do anything. Jesus retains all authority over each of us, and each of us will be accountable for what we have done or not done. We are not held responsible for what others do. We are only held responsible for those actions we do or do not do.

Authority over Our Children

While we are not to parent other adults, parents are uniquely responsible for their children. The Scriptures have a great deal to say about the relationship of parents and children. Children are commanded to honor their parents; parents are told to guide, lead, serve, and teach their children about God and his ways.

The Scriptures provide a great deal of instruction about boundary setting for our children. The Bible uses the word discipline. In both the Old and New Testaments, the most common words translated into English as discipline mean instruct, teach, and train.[20] The concept of control is not a part of the meaning of discipline. Teaching

---

20. At times the meaning is nuanced to include chastise (severely criticize) or rebuke (express strong disapproval.)

right values, both in belief and behavior, is critical and can come in many forms. The author and seasoned therapist, Jerry Beare, writes, "Children gain a sense of love from discipline, security from boundaries, respect from consistency, self-worth from contribution, and a sense of commitment from sacrifice."[21] Beare also asserts when kids are wild, insolent, and unruly, they are not "out of control," rather, they are "in control of the family." This attempt to control requires parental intervention to restore the proper parent-child relationship. It is not to be done with anger. Paul writes to the Christians in Ephesus, "Fathers, do not provoke your children to anger, but bring them up in the discipline and instruction of the Lord" (Eph 6:4). This is not to say a corrected child will not get angry, only that we are not to provoke anger. We are to parent with love and authority.

Discipline must be distinguished from punishment. Punishment is payment for doing something wrong in the past. Punishment leads us to look back and reflect on the past actions and has little impact on the future behavior. In contrast, discipline promotes the vision of looking ahead seeking to sharpen our decision-making so in the future we and our children will make wiser choices. Cloud and Townsend write, "The lessons we learn from discipline help us not to make the same mistakes again: 'God disciplines us for our good, that we may share in his holiness' (Heb 12:10)."[22]

Parents are never directly responsible for the choices their kids make, unless the parents have neglected to give the children wise guidance. However, we often bear the consequences of bad decisions they make. We pay for the neighbor's window, when our child throws a baseball through it. We might lose sleep because friends of our kids might be unruly, while they are staying with us for the weekend. While we certainly do not own our children, we are given the responsibility to bring them up with good values, knowing God, especially as they observe us living our lives.

---

21. Jerry Beare, *Parenting: A View from the Therapist's Chair* (Franklin, OH: Wolfetales Publishing, 2009), 33-34.
22. Cloud and Townsend, *Boundaries,* 180.

False Authority of Enmeshment with God

If we are enmeshed with God, we can operate out of an illegitimate sense of authority from God. We might implement acts ourselves and assert "divine guidance" to those around us. Countless errors have been made by people who believed and lived as if they had a direct hot-line to God.

Sociology professor Ronald Enroth discusses Frank Sandford whose "Christian" community led to starvation for many while he lived an opulent lifestyle. Of Sanford, he said, "The source of Sandford's unquestioned authority was God. Interpreting God's will was not left to chance since God spoke directly to Sandford.... His words and decisions became synonymous with God's."[23] Other well-known spiritual leaders such as David Koresh and Jim Jones along with a number of famous television evangelists have promoted the idea that what they say and do is a direct word and instruction from God which must be carefully followed. But, this book is not about these well-known religious cult leaders. Let us focus on people who tell that such a direct connection with God is their norm. These individuals often pray about a decision and rely upon some internal voice they believe is God's direct, individual guidance. Sometimes, such perceptions of God's direct revelations can be authentic, but many such discernments have proven unreliable. Visions of unleashed egos and countless disastrous financial decisions reveal that hyperconfidence in our listening process to God can be problematic. This is why we need healthy differentiated relationships to find what others are perceiving as God's direction, not just our own "hotline."

Enmeshment with God surfaces when we consider our discernment infallible and especially should we attempt to impose it upon others. This sense can be quite unconscious with a sense of strong passion, or it can be driven by a sense of being bestowed this role by God to direct the lives of others. Any direction we provide

---

23. Ronald M. Enroth, *Churches that Abuse* (Grand Rapids, MI: Zondervan Publishing House, 1993), 63.

must be aligned with God's calling, not simply our personal preferences. Far too often, Christians have confused their own voice and God's. If present, this enmeshment with God, like all enmeshment, will tempt us to make countless presumptions and errors in judgment. God does prompt and lead us with his divine guidance, but it is wise to maintain a certain level of tenuousness in our discernment process.

As we assess God's guidance in our selves, we should approach this assessment cautiously. Attributing anything to God that is not from him can establish an inflated security for us, sometimes leading us and others to mistaken reliance. The preponderance of God's guidance for Christ-followers comes from the Scriptures and especially from the Scriptures shared in community with other believers. There we learn how God desires his people to live, especially as they relate to God and others.

Whether we are listening to the Holy Spirit or to the Bible, we must guard against any enmeshment we have with God, especially if we see our leadership as an exercise of authority. As we become more differentiated, we develop increasing freedom to more carefully weigh the possibilities. We might even consider diversified thinking. Also, we might well change our minds on some of the issues over time, due to our experiences, wise advice from trusted friends including wise supportive leaders, and deeper understanding from study of the Scriptures. Hearing and discerning God's leading in our lives comes about through multiple means. God has proactively engaged with us to lead us in our discernment process by providing us with the Scriptures, the counsel of other Christians, and the reality of God's Holy Spirit to move upon our heart.

Closing Thoughts on Authority

While we must be accountable to the authority of those who employ us; we also have authority over the business performance of those we employ. The managers are stewards of the businesses they own and manage. Within the church, biblical authority relates to the spiritual leaders who oversee the doctrines and practices of the church and business matters. This authority, however, does not translate to personal authority over or personal management of other adults' private lives. The limit of our exhortation to others is to be disclosure and warning when a major destructive action is seen.

There can be spiritual abuse in churches and families where one person has "ascended to the throne" and crowned themselves a king of that environment. This behavior is not the proper meaning or use of biblical authority in the church or home. Here is one case of shameful spiritual abuse. One of the elders in a church had left a message for the pastor that he would not be at an important meeting. Before the meeting had been scheduled, the elder had arranged a vacation with several friends who had rearranged their schedules and booked their travel plans. The pastor was angry with the elder, even though these circumstances were not the the fault of any one person. The pastor called the elder into his office and confronted him, asking, "How can you take a vacation when we have this important meeting coming up?" To add insult to injury, the pastor had asked a second elder to attend his meeting with this elder, without alerting him to the circumstances.

The pastor accused the first elder of being unfaithful to his commitment, and shamed him for his "rebellious behavior." The pastor implied the second elder also took issue with him being away, which was not true. The confronted elder was crushed. His ability to continue worshiping with this pastor was compromised. He eventually left the church, though he had been a member much longer than the young pastor. The pastor never missed a heartbeat; he went on in the same way managing people's personal lives and leaving lots of devastated individuals behind in the process. Unfortunately, neither elder talked to the other about this encounter for a number of years. Eventually the second elder made contact with the elder who had been confronted and asked for forgiveness for participating in such an abusive process. The first elder was incredibly blessed to have his hurt validated by the other elder. Even after so many years, this apology provided a great deal of healing for both persons.

If either elder would have had a stronger and more differentiated self during the meeting with the pastor, the situation could have been avoided. They would have realized the truth of Galatians 6, while we are responsible *to* our brother and sisters, we are not responsible *for* them. The elder had properly exercised his responsibility to let the pastor know of his absence, but the pastor should have never taken the position to decide for the elder that the elders must cancel his vacation plans, and thereby impacting the elder as well as several other persons. Had the either of the elders been more differentiated, both elders would have been liberated from the dictatorial, abusive behavior of the pastor.

Even though there are many abuses of authority, this reality does not mean all authority is negative and should be rejected. There are proper expressions of authority and these are a blessing. Authority that is voluntarily attributed to someone out of love and respect for them and especially due to their spiritual and emotional maturity can have a great positive impact on people. A Christian professor, Richard, learned his life would be ending in the not too distant future due to several debilitating diseases. Anyone who knew Richard would have been thrilled to have him as a close friend. Richard invited a friend out to dinner and told him of his plight. He said, "God has put you on my heart, and I want you to know I will be available to you as long as I am physically able. You can ask me about anything, and I will disclose what I know, believe, and feel. You will have my confidence. I will never impose upon your goodness, because I will go just as far as you wish to go in our friendship. I have had a good, long life knowing God and want to share anything from my life that might be helpful and encourage you. You take the initiative, and I will always respond to you." The friend took Richard at his word and for the next year and a half had a rich friendship with Richard, asking many questions that he might never have brought up without such an invitation. Richard's death was very sad, but the friend was greatly blessed by the access Richard had given him to probe, ask questions, and learn. Their close relationship was possible because Richard understood what it meant to bear someone else's burden. The friend welcomed the authoritative wisdom that Richard provided him. There was never any hint of control or pressure. Their long conversations were life-changing for this young man.

The most persuasive use of authority is not wielded as a supervisor, but as a servant and encourager as Richard was. The Scriptures teach us to encourage one another, to build up each other, to stir each other to love and good works, and to do so gently.[24] Again and again we must reaffirm Paul's teaching of mercy to the Galatians, "Bear one another's burdens, and so fulfill the law of Christ" (Gal 6:2). This is the biblical model of authority and spiritual leadership for those within the Kingdom of God.

---

24. 1 Thes 5:11, Eph 4:29, Heb 10:24-25, and Prov 15:4.

Chapter 8

Moving into Liberation

When we make a constructive change in our dysfunctional behavior toward others, many times our relationships will seem to initially become worse, not better. We upset the pattern of our past behavior. The more people are enmeshed with us or we are with them, the more uncomfortable the relationship will become with changes in our actions. If the other person is disconnected, the person might consider our actions irrelevant to them. Emotional freedom always comes at a price. Our work is always on ourselves, not seeking to reshape those persons who are not healthily connected to us. We become stronger as we become less enmeshed and more differentiated. Licensed Therapist Dr. Jan Dunn summarized the family systems theory which can apply to all relationships with these paradoxical thoughts:

> If one wants to work on a relationship, one must work on oneself.
>
> If one wants to work on individuality, it is best done in relationship with others.
>
> In order to be less distant, one must develop better boundaries.

> In order to be less fused [enmeshed], one must develop better boundaries.[1]

We are the primary beneficiary of our emotional growth. But, the other person is as well, whether or not they see or want it.

Enmeshment Is against God's Design

In an enmeshed system of relationships, the enmeshed person lives to enhance the system of relationships. Something as virtuous sounding as "family first" turns out to trump all other things. In such a system family comes before God, before friends, before justice, virtue, moral judgment, reason, facts, and reality. It can also mean the family is more important than any individual family member's needs. The Kingdom of God is fundamentally opposed to this type of behavior.

The first element of this misguided principle is its failure to grasp the end purpose for God's creation of humanity. We understand God created the earth and all his creatures, including humankind *ex nihilo*—out of nothing. We believe he did not simply reorganize existing elements he found to make his vast creation of earth, sky, and life. He did not create the world out of a personal need for fellowship or praise by his creation. He brought forth his creation out of love. John writes, "God is love" (1 John 4:8b and 1 John 4:16a). Fundamental to God's essence is love. He did not create us to "die to self;" he created us to *be* a self. The term "dying to self" is not a biblical expression. The concept usually connotes emptying one's self from your individual desires and preferences. This understanding frames all of our desires as sinful or destructive. Many desires are given to us directly by God. In Mark 3:34, we are called to deny ourselves and follow Christ. This means we are to turn away from destructive actions that surface because of us not walking

---

1. Dunn attributes these paradoxes as taught by Dr. Glen Jennings, Cornaro professor emeritus of family sciences at Texas Woman's University. Insert added by the author., accessed November 30, 2017, https://www.drjandunn.com/blog/family-of-origin-gems/.

with God and embrace the good actions that God has desired for us to undertake. Any need to "die to self" is a result of our sin and actually means we are to die to our *false* self or *fallen* self. Humanity has become enslaved to what the Bible calls sin. The apostle Paul writes, "for all have sinned and fall short of the glory of God" (Rom 3:23). Sadly, we have given up our freedom. To regain that freedom, we need to have our hearts and lives restored to how God originally created humanity. This restoration is offered to us through the work of Jesus Christ as we respond to him. God does not ask us to eliminate our free self, nor will he ever violate this freedom. He does ask us to love one another with it. We are created to love one another.[2]

Freedom is the second foundational point that is at odds with enmeshment, which opposes God's design of his kingdom. An enmeshed system is driven by the needs of society and built upon multiple obligations. Each member of an enmeshed system is obligated to serve the whole, and expectations for each member are based on the collective needs rather than what an individual needs. Where enmeshment characterizes a community, each person in that community is obligated to give whatever is needed to remain close to the community. If an individual is unable or chooses not to do so, those within the enmeshed system will see the differentiated person as the problem.[3] Within this emotional structure, there is little or no room for individual freedom of choice without adverse consequences.

Looking at what we know about Jesus' relationship to his Father and humankind's relationship to God, freedom is one of the most important things God desires to preserve for people. God allows evil, injustice, and suffering in the world. God was willing to

---

2. Rom 12:10, 1 Thes 4:9-10, 1 Pet 1:22-24, 1 Pet 4:8, 1 John 3:11, 1 John 3:23, 1 John 4:7, 1 John 4:11-12, and 2 John 5:5.

3. Counselors often use the term "identified patient" for someone who has been designated as the scapegoat. This approach gives the dysfunctional persons in a group a way to "avoid their own internal pain disappointments, and struggles, by pointing the finger at someone else as the cause for all the problems they experience. Accessed November 18, 2017, https://lonerwolf.com/identified-patient-black-sheep/.

become human, to suffer and die for us. God is continually willing to suffer rejection by men and women, even to their own detriment, for the purpose of ensuring our choice to say "no" to God.

If we have no freedom, we cannot love. Love is the hallmark of those who follow Christ. God loves us by offering us freedom, and he often experiences suffering as a consequence of that freedom. He loves by voluntarily giving himself to us and allowing us to choose whether or not we want a relationship with him. John records what Jesus said about his own life, "No one takes it from me, but I lay it down of my own accord. I have authority to lay it down, and I have authority to take it up again" (John 10:18). Jesus freely chose to embrace his role as the one whose life, death, and resurrection was carried out for the benefit of all those who follow him. Enmeshment puts people under obligation to give what is needed, rather than extending an invitation to which we are free to respond as we choose. This obligation is squarely at odds with how God desires for us to live.[4]

As we come to understand we are enmeshed with other people or organizations, we must learn to recognize this destructive condition and take steps to assume responsibility for our decisions, making them based on our own values. Remember, enmeshment is a counterfeit substitute for authentic intimacy and faithfulness, because it does not allow one the freedom to disengage when necessary. Only when we are free to choose to do or not to do something are we living a balanced life.

Emancipation from Enmeshment

Enmeshment can take three forms. We can be enmeshed with another person, or they can be enmeshed with us. The third and most difficult strain of enmeshment to break is when there is reciprocal

---

4. This blog post by Anna Lynn was particularly helpful to the author in focusing on the issue of enmeshment being against God's design. Accessed December 29, 2017, https://thoughtsbyannalynn.wordpress.com/2013/07/04/eneshment-and-the-kingdom-of-god/

enmeshment with another person. A great place to begin to eliminate enmeshment with others is to look for signs of enmeshment in our life. Name the person you are considering, and identify what boundaries of theirs you are upholding that are in conflict with your own values. Also, identify boundaries of yours they do not respect. Begin to act responsibly toward them as an adult. We give them a safe space with us and withhold our judgments about their behavior, unless we are asked to provide them. We strive to cease seeing them as an extension of ourself.

As we identify enmeshment we have with others, strive to replace that feeling with thanks to God that he has created us unique, yet also in his image. Celebrate our uniqueness. We can seek to identify a personal mentor who we observe as well-differentiated and share with them our struggles of enmeshment or disconnection. Listen to his or her life experiences and learn from their healthy emotional habits. When we are fortunate enough to have several great friends, we do not need to try to make ourselves into the persons we most admire. One way to assess our level of freedom from enmeshment is whether or not we feel the freedom to direct our own decisions.

Narcissism is a form of extreme selfishness, in which someone has a grossly inflated view of themselves resulting from a failure to distinguish the self from external objects, in many cases another person who admires them. When relating to someone who is enmeshed with us, that relationship can appeal to the latent narcissism which is present in almost all of us.

To establish long-term stability and give others the opportunity to reduce their enmeshment with us, make your intentional boundaries clear to them. We must not waiver in what we communicate. Resist the temptation to please them by violating your stated boundaries. If you do not work on weekends, do not answer the business phone or respond to email on weekends, short of an emergency. We must be clear, but polite, not manipulative or abusive. Give others the freedom to make their own decisions. Should you find yourself involved with enmeshment in any of these three ways, the only path to your liberation is to change how you relate with the other persons and live without enmeshment.

Liberation from Disconnection

When we have been emotionally scarred by someone's actions, we may want to punish that person. The apostle Peter spoke in opposition to this thinking, when he wrote this about Jesus, "When they hurled their insults at him, he did not retaliate; when he suffered, he made no threats. Instead, he entrusted himself to him who judges justly" (1 Pet 2:23). Paul also addressed this subject in his letter to the Roman Christians where he wrote,

> Repay no one evil for evil, but give thought to do what is honorable in the sight of all. If possible, so far as it depends on you, live peaceably with all. Beloved, never avenge yourselves, but leave it to the wrath of God, for it is written, "Vengeance is mine, I will repay, says the Lord." To the contrary, "if your enemy is hungry, feed him; if he is thirsty, give him something to drink; for by so doing you will heap burning coals on his head." Do not be overcome by evil, but overcome evil with good. (Rom 12:17-21)

Be slow to voice your disagreements with others. Before you launch an attack, consider asking questions such as, "Could you restate your thoughts on the matter?" Ask if you can restate what you heard, without judgments, to make certain you fully understand their perspective. Ask questions such as, "Why is this important to you?" Perhaps indicate you will get back to them after considering the matter a bit more. Retaliation has no place in the Christian's behavior. Do not confuse retaliation with the idea of establishing a clear strong boundary for protection. Making an assertive intervention to break an ongoing pattern of abuse can be a redemptive response to our Christian friends as long as we are not retaliating out of vengeance.

When we know there is a strong disconnection, seek reconciliation early on. If we believe we are at fault, ask for forgiveness. If we do not believe we are at fault, ask them to express their feelings and listen in an effort to uncover their point of view. If we are not able to state their position in such a manner, without judgments, so they can affirm our words as an accurate summation of their feelings, we do not yet understand their point of view. This is particularly difficult, although critically important, when we strongly disagree with someone. Continued communication is always important. Retaliatory behavior followed by emotional disconnection is one approach that will guarantee our relationship will have no reconciliation and, therefore, no hope of becoming differentiated.

In spite of that person's behavior, at some point we must be willing to take the risk of moving toward the person who has wounded us, if any significant reconciliation is to occur. It is important that we carefully consider our next steps in the process. The old adage "forgive and forget" should not be embraced without considerable caution. I would recommend a revised edition of this expression: "forgive and remember." Edith Stauffer explains, "…we need to remember the situation to protect ourselves in the future. However, we do not remember the act to use it against another; we remember it only to learn from it."[5]

When we sense a progression of disconnection, we need to seek out a group where we can seek advice, counseling, and encouragement toward emotional health. Recognize that some relationships cannot be restored as long as the other person is unwilling to talk and process the disconnection. In those rare situations, there is not much else we can do to restore the relationship. Remember, the act of forgiveness is always ours alone. The other person plays no part in that process.[6] Reconciliation, however, requires both parties to meet and be committed to a future relationship. If we have repeatedly initiated

---

5. Edith R. Stauffer, *Unconditional Love and Forgiveness* (Diamond Springs, CA: Triangle Publishers, 1987), 204.
6. Ellis, *Forgiveness*, 27.

and the other person refuses to process the conflict with us, the beauty of a differentiated lifestyle remains even when we are unable to achieve reconciliation. We need not assume the responsibility for that problem. Learning to move forward without reconciliation in some situations is the only way to find peace within ourselves.

Balance Individuality and Togetherness

Even an emotionally healthy individual experiences a tension between two forces that pull against each other: individuality and togetherness. The desire for togetherness urges us toward one another. We desire secure attachment, being a part of something bigger than we are. We like to receive affirmation, validation, and approval from others we respect. We can draw strength from family and friends when our relationships are healthy. These important forces, when in healthy balance, can give us strengthening connection with others.

The force of individuality helps us define our self as separate from others. This important force empowers us to form individual beliefs and establish personal autonomy. Individuation, the work of forming a strong self with our own ideas, preferences, agendas, and goals, results in our becoming distinct from other people. Individuality is supported by having personal boundaries that are non-negotiable in our relationships.[7]

It can be challenging to live drawing from both of these forces with some internal sense of centeredness. At times, we yearn for one or the other which we feel might be lacking at that point in our life. A married person might long for the sense of independence that can sometimes be more easily lived out in singleness, unencumbered with the responsibilities of a spouse and children. A single person might long for the type of connectedness they believe is fundamental with married couples. One who has lost a loving spouse or who has been physically or emotionally wounded by a partner, resulting

---

7. Gilbert, *Extraordinary Relationships*, 13-14.

in separation or divorce, can have difficulty refocusing their life and reach more into a healthy level of togetherness. Establishing a centeredness from each of these life-changing arenas can come about only through substantial work on one's self. Many people find great help from a skilled counselor or a well-differentiated friend with whom they can be transparent.

Separate, Equal, and Open

There are no perfect individuals. Certainly, there are no perfect relationships. However, there are many people that have great relationships with others. Psychiatrist Roberta Gilbert writes there are three necessary elements required for ideal, healthy relationships. Healthy relationships are made of people who are separate, equal, and open.[8] The absence of any one of these three elements will pose significant obstacles to forming a healthy, balanced relationship.

By separate we mean we must neither draw from nor provide the self for the other person in our relationship. Emotionally healthy people probably have a little more individuality than a requirement for togetherness, but we need a balance of both. Emotionally healthy relationships will usually be found primarily between differentiated people. Healthy persons are less likely to become enmeshed with other persons. We must have a clear understanding of who we are and what boundaries we require others to respect. In addition, we must have a willingness to honor the boundaries of the other person. Emotionally healthy people are not dependent upon other persons for their emotional happiness. We may choose to bring emotional encouragement to another, but we do so freely and intentionally, not out of a sense of obligation. We are separate but not isolated.

By equal, I do not mean equivalent or the same. Healthy relationships must be on equal footing. Equality is not contracted by listing the strengths each of us bring to the relationship in equal-proportion. It means in our functioning relationship there is mutual

---

8. Ibid., 110, 159.

respect. Each person sees the other as talented, responsible, and able to operate independently of the other and is encouraged to do so. We may divide up responsibilities to conquer a task, but important decisions are mutually agreeable. Conversations are highly valued because of the respect and honor that we have for one another. There is no embedded exercise of power or authority by either person over the other.

Finally, healthy relationships are open to change by both people. We listen to the other person, giving freedom for sharing a different perspective, and we learn to understand things from their point of view. We provide a safe space for disclosure of their feelings and perceptions. Only then can we decide whether or not we agree with the other person. Should we disagree, we remain differentiated and continue to disclose. The other person listens to our concerns and perspective, as well, without judging us. Operating this way is the opposite of being emotionally shut down or cut off from the other person. In all our interactions with others, we continually engage in an ongoing dialogue. The animation in our voice, facial expressions, eye contact, physical gestures, and postures all carry our feelings back and forth, even when they are unspoken.[9] Openness can be a challenge when one is working to restore a relationship, especially if one or both of the persons has been emotionally wounded by the other over a long period of time. Any tendency to withdraw from openness in the relationship and move toward disconnection will begin to erode the relationship. In a healthy relationship, one takes the risk of continuing to disclose because the relationship is safe and important to us.

Embracing Differentiation Is Challenging

Differentiation is a learned skilled, a way of living one's life without being easily manipulated by others. If we recognize we have been living a life of either substantial enmeshment or disconnection,

---

9. Ibid., 105.

we may have advanced past the first positive step toward differentiation. As we establish boundaries, both within ourselves and regarding how we will be treated and we learn how to respect the boundaries of other people, the shift can be difficult. Accept the reality that transitioning from either an enmeshed or disconnected relationship will be a great deal of work, when we begin relating to the other person in a more healthy way. We can often expect push-back from those who are no longer receiving from us what they want. The more enmeshed they are with us, the more likely their feelings will be hurt, because we have now changed. Expect to face multiple obstacles and continue our learning process. Sometimes this process can take a long time.

Build relationships with people you believe are well-differentiated. This transformation in how we think, feel, and live will be challenging but also rewarding. High-quality professional counseling can provide a safe space with a differentiated person to help facilitate your desired changes in thinking and behavior. Remember, we are the ones who ultimately make the assessments of both your counselor and your process of spiritual and psychological growth. As you read through the appendix of this book, you will learn about several different approaches to counseling which can be great help in growing into emotional adulthood. Hopefully, what you read there will assist you to make an informed choice about when and where to seek assistance.

Concluding Thoughts about Healthy Relationships

As you recall the many characters in the short stories from the first chapter of this book, you can now look back and identify many of the dysfunctions present in their behavior—bad boundaries that lead to enmeshment with others, as well as disconnection from people with whom they can no longer tolerate. As we come to grips with the reality that to have better relationships with others, we must work on ourselves. Resist the temptation to react in dysfunctional ways when we are offended. Never let someone else's bad behavior dictate how we respond to them. As we move forward, some relationships might become more conflicted initially. With time and practice the more healthy pattern will provide increasing stability for us as we develop a more differentiated lifestyle.

I close this chapter with a final true story about a person whose life dramatically changed, because he changed. John was seen by all who knew him as a good man—one who was faithful to his wife, attended church regularly, taught Bible classes, did not cheat on his taxes, and worked hard at providing a safe space for his family to live. His wife was very expressive and full of life. John wanted to provide all she wanted to make her happy. He did the best he could in these areas. On many levels, he was successful at doing just that. However, the one thing she wanted the most was for him to know her, emotionally see her, and for him to share his heart with her. This type of sharing by him was absent in their relationship. He had absolutely no idea how to do that. When she talked about wanting "to be seen," John felt she was speaking a foreign language to him. This grave shortcoming almost cost him his marriage.

He was plenty smart and well-educated. But he was clueless about deep, personal differentiated relationships. He went away to a special event where he was forced to break the mold and begin to share his feelings. He obtained the courage to move into unfamiliar spaces and take the risks of participating in team events and discussions, engaging in experiences that gave him the vision and courage to speak up. A major decision came after three months in this life-changing men's movement. He made a decision to enter graduate school and study Christian history and theology. There, he moved into a new, expansive worldview that was dramatically beyond anything he knew existed. He is now on a life-long journey of a Christian transformation process. He became much better connected to his wife and his family. Many good relationships became excellent relationships. Yet some damaged relationships have not been restored.

Learning to become differentiated while still loving and living with others is always a process in process. If you sense you need to define and live with stronger boundaries, I invite you to step into this process of transformation. Living a life that has a healthy balance of both independence and togetherness will provide you with incalculable freedom and greatly increased joy. Great heart connections with one another require healthy persons who know that living with good boundaries means loving within limits between individuality and connectedness. If you need help with this process, I encourage you to find it.

Appendix
Approaches to Counseling and Scripture

Diverse Claims of Authenticity

In most professions, we have an array of resources from which we can seek advice to help guide our behavior and our hearts. If we seek to develop healthy relationships, we have our parents, a spouse, friends, pastors, counselors, psychologists, self-help books, YouTube videos, and endless free advice from countless websites and blogs. Many of these resources are driven by people with strong opinions and are founded within a particular framework. I contend no one source possesses all there is to know about how to resolve conflicts and sustain healthy relationships. Fortunately, the Scriptures present us with valuable insights that can undergird how we see ourselves, respond to God, and treat one another. Many seminaries train counselors who draw wisdom from the Bible and also use tested, extra-biblical resources that are congruent with Christian perspectives when helping others to navigate through their personal challenges. However, well-intended Christ-followers are not of one mind on the merits of drawing from psychology to help assist those who are in crisis shift to a place of resolution and spiritual stability.

There are endless ways to examine the approaches to counseling. In addition to the Scriptures, there are behavioral approaches and complex academic models from which therapists can draw their processes for help. I submit there are three broadly-based theories based on the connection between psychology and the Scriptures. These groups are not at all monolithic. Within each camp, there is a wide diversity of sources considered as authority on which one leans, approaches to counseling, and the outcomes sought by the counselor. But, most approaches will fall squarely into one of these general categories: secular counseling, biblical counseling, and holistic counseling.

Secular Counseling

This approach embodies a large variety of schools of thought and would clearly be classified as so-called secular counseling. Within this arena religious biases are deemed unscientific and not relied upon. Excluded from this stream of counseling is any looking to Scripture or prayer as a source of help. There is often an underlying assumption that stands in contrast to Christian orthodoxy, humankind is basically good, but often dysfunctional. When one's flawed behavior is discerned, the behavior can be straightened out so as to make the life less stressful for the person seeking help. This approach is primarily a way of shifting your mind to embrace a particular way of thinking, which will not include any particular spiritual framework.

Often, a therapist will discuss points of previous trauma in the person's life and help reframe the situation to feel less painful. This process can be seen as a freedom from these bad traumas. These traumas are not reconsidered as good, rather a temporary return to them simply allows the therapist to guide the client to learn something constructive from their being victimized or for their making an unwise choice. There are dozens of schools of thoughts that look to this approach for counseling. Many counselors would rely upon psychoanalysis developed by people such as Sigmund Freud, Alfred Alder, and Carl Jung, along with dozens of other processes such as Transactional Analysis, est (Ehard Seminar Training), Gestalt, and hypnotherapy.

In recent years many secular-based therapists have shifted somewhat away from these early models for counseling and focus primarily upon how one can modify their actual behavior. With this approach a client is taught about tools one can use to compensate for innate deficiencies and help the client move away from areas where they are stuck in destructive behaviors. This approach can sometimes bring about desired behavioral changes more rapidly than using the earlier approaches to counseling. Many therapists draw from several different approaches, combining them as they deem appropriate for the particular individual they are counseling.

Biblical Counseling

Certain counselors reject counseling not based exclusively on the Bible. They identify themselves as "biblical counselors" or nouthetic counselors.[1] These counselors reject the research and guidance offered by what they classify as secular theories. One of the primary proponents of this approach to counseling is Jay Adams. Adams writes,

> Rather than defer and refer to psychiatrists steeped in their humanistic dogma, ministers of the gospel and other Christian workers who have been called by God to help his people out of their distress, will be encouraged to reassume their privileges and responsibilities. Shall they defer and refer? Only as an exception, never as the rule, and then only to other more competent Christian workers. Their task is to *confer*. The thesis of this book [Adams' book, *Competent to Counsel*] is that qualified Christian counselors properly trained in the Scriptures are competent to counsel—more competent than psychiatrists or anyone else.[2]

---

1. The term nouthetic counseling comes from the Greek word, *noutheteo*, which means to admonish. It is a form of Evangelical Protestant counseling based solely upon the Bible and focused on Christ. It repudiates mainstream psychology and psychiatry as humanistic, radically secular, and fundamentally opposed to Christianity.
2. Jay E. Adams, *Competent to Counsel* (Nutley NJ: Presbyterian and Reformed Publishing Co., 1970), 18.

Adams continues, "Nouthetic confrontation always implies a problem, and presupposes an obstacle that must be overcome; something is wrong in the life of the one who is confronted."[3] "Nouthetic confrontation, in the biblical usage, aims at straightening out the individual by changing his patterns of behavior to conform to biblical standards."[4] Adams declares nouthetic counselors are more interested in modifying a client's behavior than in exploring why he or she feels that way.

Proponents of this counseling approach teach "the Bible addresses every 'dysfunction' and presents the essential truths required to bring humans into full maturity."[5] They partly defend this understanding by incorrectly looking at Paul's letter to Timothy, where he wrote, "All Scripture is breathed out by God and profitable for teaching, for reproof, for correction, and for training in righteousness, that the man of God may be complete, equipped for every good work" (2 Tim 3:16-17). The assertion is the Bible declares if one submits to the disciplines and prescriptions put forth in the Old and New Testament Scriptures, then one will become more and more perfected, eventually complete. When Paul made reference to the Scripture in the text above, in all probability he was not talking about the Bible we now have. Actually, Paul was most likely speaking about the five honored books of Jewish Law, the *Torah* (the first five books of the Old Testament). They were compiled in the sixth to fourth centuries BC, while the rest of the Old Testament was just beginning to function as an unofficial canon of Hebrew Scripture by the AD 70s, after Paul's death. Paul is believed to have been "decapitated under Nero between the years 65 and 67."[6] Much of the New Testament was not yet written, and what was written was definitely not widely circulated and universally read at that point in time.

---

3. Ibid., 44.
4. Ibid., 46.
5. Ed Bulkley, *Why Christians Can't Trust Psychology,* (Eugene OR: Harvest House Publishers. 1993), 29.
6. Walter A. Elwell and Barry J. Beitzel, *Baker Encyclopedia of the Bible* (Grand Rapids, MI: Baker Book House, 1988), 1633.

Lest we be overly dogmatic on this point, we must understand Peter recorded, "And count the patience of our Lord as salvation, just as our beloved brother Paul also wrote to you according to the wisdom given to him, as he does in all his letters when he speaks in them of these matters. There are some things in them that are hard to understand, which the ignorant and unstable twist to their own destruction, as they do the other Scriptures" (2 Pet 3:15-16). Peter considered Paul's letters that were being circulated at the time of his ministry to be Scripture. In addition, Paul wrote to Timothy, "For the Scripture says, 'You shall not muzzle an ox when it treads out the grain" and "the laborer deserves his wages'" (1Tim 5:18). The first part of this passage is quoted from Deuteronomy 25:4, but the last part is from Luke 10:7. Perhaps, by inference we might understand Paul to have thought the book of Luke as Scripture. With these two examples from the New Testament, it is clear there were at least isolated cases where the writings of some of the apostles were eventually considered on par with the Jewish Scriptures. But, it would be quite presumptive to infer Paul was referring to what we now have as our New Testament, since most of it was yet to be written, and it was not yet agreed upon by church leaders what would and would not be included and identified as Scripture.[7]

It was early in the second century, long after Paul's death, when Christ-followers "began to treat certain specifically Christian writings as equal to the Jewish Scriptures."[8] Looking at all this information, I believe the preponderance of evidence concerning the 2 Timothy passage, as I stated earlier, Paul was likely referring to what we know as the *Torah*, which he considered profitable for forming our Christian character. I am not saying the Scriptures of all the Old Testament and New Testaments are not profitable to us, only that

---

7. Jeroslav Pelikan, *Whose Bible Is it? A Short History of the Scriptures* (London: Penguin Books, 2004), 115-117.
8. Mark Allan Powell, "Canon," in *The HarperCollins Bible Dictionary* (Revised and Updated), ed. Mark Allan Powell (New York: HarperCollins, 2011), 120.

Paul was speaking only of the *Torah*. Furthermore, if you read in an earlier letter to Timothy from Paul, we learn the church of God, not the Scriptures, is the anchor and pier or foundation of truth. Writing about church leadership he declares, "They must hold the mystery of the faith with a clear conscience. And let them also be tested first; then let them serve as deacons if they prove themselves blameless" (1 Tim 3:9-10). Paul continues, "I hope to come to you soon, but I am writing these things to you so that, if I delay, you may know how one ought to behave in the household of God, which is the church of the living God, a pillar and buttress of the truth. Great indeed, we confess, is the mystery of godliness: He [Jesus] was manifested in the flesh, vindicated by the Spirit, seen by angels, proclaimed among the nations, believed on in the world, taken up in glory" (1 Tim 3:14-16).

Part of our Christian faith embraces the church, not the Scriptures alone, as a pillar and buttress of the truth. The imagery of the church being a pillar or buttress places the community of Christ-followers as the containers of truth and is the testimony to one another and the world of the truth of the gospel of Jesus Christ. The mystery of godliness is also God's design for our redemption. In verse 17 we read, "...that the man of God may be complete, equipped for every good work" (1 Tim 3:17). This does not mean we can become perfect or all-knowing, which is reserved for God alone; the word for complete and the word for equipped are synonyms. This verse means we can be proficient, fully equipped for whatever God calls us to do.[9]

Also, these "biblical counselors" look to the writings of Peter: "His divine power has granted to us *all things*[10] that pertain to life and godliness, through the knowledge of him who called us to his own glory and excellence, by which he has granted to us his precious and very great promises, so that through them you may become partakers of the divine nature, having escaped from the corruption that is in the world because of sinful desire" (2 Pet 1:3-4). One of the

---

9. Daniel C. Arichea and Howard Hatton, *A Handbook on Paul's Letters to Timothy and to Titus* (New York: United Bible Societies, 1995), 237.
10. Italics added by the author.

primary ways we gain knowledge of God is by reading the Scriptures. But, Peter is definitely not writing specifically about Scripture. Instead, he is writing about character of Christ-followers that exhibits the nature of what God is like (*imago dei*). The Bible does not claim to address every specific problem that humankind faces. It is important to note Peter continues by declaring knowledge of God and his gift of grace toward us is not sufficient for our transformation to which God calls us. Like Paul, Peter declares we are to remain faithful and live a Godly life. He writes,

> For this very reason, make every effort to supplement your faith with virtue, and virtue with knowledge, and knowledge with self-control, and self-control with steadfastness, and steadfastness with godliness, and godliness with brotherly affection, and brotherly affection with love. For if these qualities are yours and are increasing, they keep you from being ineffective or unfruitful in the knowledge of our Lord Jesus Christ. For whoever lacks these qualities is so nearsighted that he is blind, having forgotten that he was cleansed from his former sins. Therefore, brothers, be all the more diligent to confirm your calling and election, for if you practice these qualities you will never fall. For in this way there will be richly provided for you an entrance into the eternal kingdom of our Lord and Savior Jesus Christ. Therefore I intend always to remind you of these qualities, though you know them and are established in the truth that you have. (2 Pet 1:5-12)

The Bible is God's special revelation to humanity about himself and his relationship with us. It does not make any claim to contain all the knowledge and wisdom of life we are to discover. While what is in the Scripture it true and trustworthy, Scripture is neither exhaustive nor, according to Peter, is knowledge of its instruction singularly adequate for our spiritual maturation. The Bible is not a book of science. While it records historic events, it is not primarily a history book. It is not a medical book or a book about mathematics. It is not a book about financial management, nutrition, or political or social structuring, although it presents truths on all these subjects. Therefore, framing the Scriptures as containing all the direct truth and guidance for our lives puts them into a perspective neither the Scriptures nor history affirm.

Francis Schaeffer offers a helpful perspective on the authority of Scripture:

> We are considering here matters which lie far in the past and concern cosmic events. That raises a question: Can we really talk in any meaningful sense at all about them? It is helpful, first, to distinguish between true communication and exhaustive communication. What we claim as Christians is that when all of the facts are taken into consideration, the Bible gives us true knowledge although not exhaustive knowledge. Man as a finite creature is incapable of handling exhaustive knowledge anyway. There is an analogy here with our own communication between men; we communicate to each other truly, but we do not communicate exhaustively. A Christian holding the strongest possible view of inspiration still does not claim exhaustive knowledge at any point.[11]

Holistic Counseling

The third counseling approach is called holistic counseling. In one way or another this approach values both exhortation and guidance from the Scriptures as well as natural revelation resources that appear congruent with what is taught in the Scriptures.[12] Within this camp, we will find people who use Scripture to reinforce assessments the counselor makes using the tools of social science. We will also find the reverse, therapists who know the Scriptures well and use examples from scientific research to further lend credibility for the

---

11. Schaeffer, *The Complete Works of Francis A. Schaeffer*, 22–23.
12. Natural revelation is the theological term for how God reveals himself through his creation. This is as opposed to special revelation which would be through a prophet or apostle. See Ps 19:1-6.

teachings from the Scriptures. Holistic counselors look to the specific revelation of God through the Scriptures, but also to the general revelation of God through humanity and the creation. Paul addresses this in his writing to the church in Rome: "For his invisible attributes, namely, his eternal power and divine nature, have been clearly perceived, ever since the creation of the world, in the things that have been made. So they are without excuse" (Rom 1:20). The general nature of God is also revealed in his creation. This holistic approach is taught in many Christian colleges and seminaries throughout the world. The goal of holistic counseling is not simply to modify one's behavior. The counselor explores why a person is driven to behave a certain way and strives to help uncover the means for reframing his or her decision-making in a more constructive manner.

The term *social science* is generally considered an oxymoron by biblical counselors, because many people assert we cannot treat social assessments in a scientific manner. As researchers learn how to make accurate assessments of social opinion and behavior, they discover while it is perhaps not as exact a science as electricity and gravitational studies, one can clearly quantify changes in social behavior and values when the studies follow the proper assessment process. These assessments of changes can be made for both individuals and affiliated groups.

We must be careful not to look at scientists as the caretakers of absolute truth. Scientists and engineers are pragmatic. If a theory appears to work, they embrace it, at least until a better theory is developed. For centuries the most educated rational astronomers believed the earth was flat. They believed the earth was the center of the universe and celestial bodies encircled it. The German scientist, Johannes Kepler (b. 1571, d. 1630), challenged these "truths." We now know the early astronomers were incorrect and Kepler's view replaced the old "truth." Newtonian physics was taught as truth for centuries after the Sir Isaac Newton observed the proverbial apple falling from a tree. That observation led the mathematician to postulate the idea of gravity.[13] While Newton's work still has great value, the work of Einstein brought physics to a more accurate model and laid the groundwork for what became quantum mechanics. Quantum mechanics is a fundamental shift away from the important basic formulations by Isaac Newton. It is a more complicated model for physics, but correlates better with what we see as reality.

Francis Schaeffer continues this discussion writing,

> We must not claim, on the one hand, that science is unnecessary or meaningless, nor, on the other hand, that the extensions we make from Scripture are absolutely accurate or that these extensions have the same validity as the statements of Scripture itself. But all that does not change the fact that biblical revelation is propositional, to be handled on the basis of reason in relationship to science and coordinated with science. The content of Scripture is not upper-story, and the whole of Scripture is revelational.[14]

Holistic approaches to counseling affirm that we will not always have all the answers, because our limits of understanding cannot embrace the full knowledge that God has. Schaeffer elaborates on this thought when he writes,

> As we look at the differentiations that occur when God says "Let it be this way," we can have confidence that this is true history, but that does not mean that the situation is exhaustively revealed or that all our questions are answered. This was the case with our forefathers; it is so for us and will be for everyone who comes after us. Indeed, as we stand before God in time to come, even as we see Him face to face, His communication then—certainly being more than what we now have—will still not be totally exhaustive, because we who are finite can never exhaust

---

13. See the Memoirs of Sir Isaac Newton's life by William Stukeley. The history can be read at http://ttp.royalsociety.org/ttp/ttp.html?id=1807da00-909a-4abf-b9c1-0279a08e4bf2&type=book, 15.

14. Schaeffer, *The Complete Works of Francis A. Schaeffer*, see chapter 4 of *No Final Conflict*.

the infinite. What we know can be true and normative, and yet not be a completely detailed map containing all of the knowledge which God Himself has.[15]

In the same way, social scientists understand relational models of behavior are always under examination. Some of the early social science formulations by Sigmund Freud have been substantially reframed by social scientists such as Murray Bowen, who shifted from an individualistic view of behavior to understanding individuals must understand themselves as a part of a social system relating to others. While this shift in social science is ground-breaking, we do not yet have all we need to successfully address our relational conflicts using the best of current psychological skills.

Much of how one addresses the mixture of science and Scripture is driven by one's view of the nature and purpose of the Scriptures. Christ-followers are vigilant. One school of thought is we look to the writing of Scripture as the exclusive guide for our faith and practices. We must conform our lives to what is spelled out in Scripture. We are not permitted to do things not specifically commanded in the Scriptures. Some people believe if the Scripture affirms a particular position to one group of people at one time, these instructions are implicitly understood as universal, applicable to all places, times, and cultures. Such thinking brings out the necessity of tithing[16] to the local church, prohibition of women as pastors and elders, and male authority over the wife and family. A contrasting understanding of the nature and purpose of the Scriptures is they are fully complete to reveal to us how God approaches us and how we are to respond to him. Because we live in grace, we are free to make many choices and decisions that are not in conflict with what is taught in the Scriptures. The conclusion from this point of view is we can draw from science and social sciences tools that are based on truth.

---

15. Ibid., 23–24.
16. Mandatory tithing requires ten percent of one's income being given to the local church.

Finally, the ostensible dichotomy of secular versus sacred actions promoted by some people is a false dichotomy. Our changing of a baby's messy diaper and working the night shift at a gas station can be just as sacred of an action as preaching the gospel to thousands of people or leading a praise team of musicians, when it is done from a heart that follows God. Each of these actions can be a sacred act of worship of God. The apostle Paul writes, "So, whether you eat or drink, or whatever you do, do all to the glory of God" (1 Cor 10:31). In *Radical Worship: What Sunday Morning Can Never Give You* we read,

> Internationally recognized Bach scholar Hannsdeter Wohlfarth writes, "Bach made little distinction between sacred and secular music or even sacred and secular vocations. When composing secular preludes solely for his children, he prefaced them with 'in nominee Jesus' [in the name of Jesus] just as he added "Soli Deo Gloria [to the glory of God alone] as a colophon to his religious scores.[17] Likewise, two generations later, William Wilberforce was torn between whether to serve God or remain a member of British Parliament. He sought advice from his friend, and Anglican Priest, John Newton, who suggested to him the then novel idea that Wilberforce do God's work as a member of Parliament. Wilberforce took the advice and led the movement to have slave trade abolished. After twenty-two years of battling Parliament, he succeeded in passing the Slave Trade Act in 1807.[18]

Radical Worship: What Sunday Morning Can Never Give You discusses the three unified but differentiated avenues of worship: individual worship, lifestyle worship, and community worship. It is critical that we embrace all three avenues, because each avenue brings about transformation for us in a different way.[19]

---

17. Hannsdieter Wohlfarth, *Johann Sebastian Bach* (Philadelphia: Fortress Press, 1985), book cover flap.

18. Jonathan Aitken, *John Newton: From Disgrace to Amazing Grace* (Wheaton, IL: Crossway Books, 2007), 299-317.

19. Ellis, *Radical Worship*, chapter 4.

In April, 1521, Martin Luther, a priest in the Roman Catholic church, the leader of the Reformation was confronted by at the Diet (assembly meeting of religious leaders) in Worms, Germany. Luther believed there was major corruption within the Catholic Church and had publicly declared ninety-five points of disagreement with the church leadership. He believed salvation was never earned by someone's attempt at good works, rather it was a gift to those who had faith in Jesus and what he had done on their behalf. The Church insisted that he repudiate his writings or suffer the consequence of excommunication from the Church. They understood ex-communication as eternal damnation of his soul to hell. After careful consideration, here is his response. "Unless I am convicted by Scripture and plain reason—I do not accept the authority of popes and councils, for they have contradicted each other—my conscience is captive to the Word of God. I cannot and I will not recant anything, for to go against conscience is neither right nor safe. God help me. Amen."[20] He was excommunicated from the Catholic Church. He became the chief catalyst for Protestantism. Luther was clearly differentiated from the church leadership. He looked to the Scriptures and plain reason, rather than edicts from church leaders in Rome, even though he had long been a parish priest and professor of theology in the Roman Catholic Church.

For Luther, truth was found in the Scriptures and logical reasoning, not the dogmas of the institutional Roman Catholic Church. Both Bach and Wilberforce saw no distinction between sacred and secular. Centuries ago, there was no conflict between faith and science. Science was seen as the means of discovering what God was doing with his creation. Today, many people try to pit one against the other. While Paul, Peter, and Luther cherished the Scriptures, they never withdrew from the rest of perceptions and understanding that God had provided to those who God made in his image. Paul was a high-ranking Jew and a Pharisee. He knew and highly valued the

---

20. Roland A. Banton, *Here I Stand: A Life of Martin Luther* (New York, NY: Meridian, 1955), 144.

Torah.[21] Yet, he also wrote to Timothy that the church of God was the pillar and buttress of truth. Peter tells us the true way someone knows we are a Christ-follower is by the way we live our life, exhibiting what God is like.[22]

Holistic counseling places high value on the Scripture and truths presented there about the nature of God and humanity but also values observations that we make through natural events, science, our meaningful relationships. This approach to counseling blurs the separation between what is sacred and what is secular, embracing that all we do before God is to be sacred.

The Wisdom of Counsel

When Jesus provided three different counseling sessions with three different people, even though they all asked him essentially the same question about how to obtain eternal life, he gave three very different answers. He told a Jewish religious leader he must be merciful;[23] to another Jewish man, well educated in the Hebrew Scriptures, he responded he that must sell his possessions and give the money to the poor;[24] he told Nicodemus, another prominent Jewish leader he must be born again.[25] It is interesting to note when Jesus is talking to Nicodemus about believing, he does not contrast believing against unbelief. Instead, he sees the opposite of belief as disobedience, and disobedience is what provokes God's wrath. Here, we see both a promise and a warning. John records these words of Jesus, "Whoever believes in the Son has eternal life; whoever does not obey the Son shall not see life, but the wrath of God remains on him" (John 3:36). Each person desired a life that would give them a life with God, but Jesus' counsel was explicitly focused on the needs of each one, which were different.

---

21. Acts 3:4; 9; 10:16; and 17:1-2
22. 2 Pet 1:5-12
23. Luke 10:25-37.
24. Matt 19:21-22.
25. John 3:1-26.

If we recognize some dysfunctional behaviors in our life and believe we could benefit from having a sounding board to help us move into a more differentiated lifestyle, I recommend that we advance this process with a qualified counselor. My opinion is that finding a holistic counselor would be a constructive approach. Many people start a counseling process because of a presenting problem, but with the help of a qualified therapist find that there are often other areas that impact the problem that they had not previously identified. As you take full ownership of your decisions starting with the selection of a trusted counselor, you will begin the process of healing and restoration.

As we have seen throughout this book, there are many voices that lay claim to the truth. Building healthy relationships must be based on truth not enmeshed or disconnected counterfeits of truth. As you strive to integrate your life with others in a healthy way, strive to avoid the pitfalls presented in this book. I close with one of my most treasured verses in Scripture from the book of Proverbs which reads, "Iron sharpens iron, and one man sharpens another" (Prov 27:17). Knowing this wise truth, be careful which type of man or woman you look to for your sharpening. One who is smart but disconnected will not speak to your soul. One who is enmeshed will not surface crises when examination and changes are needed. One who is well differentiated, such as Nathan, the prodigal's father, and certainly Jesus will sharpen us well.

Bibliography

Achtemeier, Paul J. *Inspiration and Authority: Nature and Function of Christian Scripture.* Peabody, MA: Hendrickson Publishers, 2005.

Adams, Jay E. *Competent to Counsel.* Nutley, NJ: Presbyterian and Reformed Publishing Co., 1970.

Aitken, Jonathan. *John Newton: From Disgrace to Amazing Grace.* Wheaton, IL: Crossway Books, 2007.

Alden, Robert L. *The New American Commentary.* Vol. 11. *Job.* Nashville: Broadman & Holman Publishers, 1993.

Arichea, Daniel C. and Howard Hatton. *A Handbook on Paul's Letters to Timothy and to Titus.* New York: United Bible Societies, 1995.

Bainton, Roland A. *Here I Stand: A Life of Martin Luther.* New York: NY: Meridian. 1955.

Beare, Jerry. *Parenting: A View from the Therapist's Chair.* Franklin, OH: Wolfetales Publishing, 2009.

Bergen, Robert D. *The New American Commentary.* Vol. 7. *1, 2 Samuel.* Nashville: Broadman & Holman Publishers, 1996.

Billings, J. Todd. *Remembrance, Communion, and Hope.* Grand Rapids, MI: William B. Eerdmans Publishing Company, 2018.

Blomberg, Craig. *Matthew*, vol. 22, The New American Commentary. Nashville: Broadman & Holman Publishers, 1992.

Borchert, Gerald L. *Galatians, Cornerstone Biblical Commentary*, vol. 14. Carol Stream, IL: Tyndale House Publishes, Inc., 2007.

Brauch, Manfred T. *Abusing Scripture.* Downers Grove, IL: InterVarsity Press, 2009.

Brown, Jeannine K. and Steven J. Sandage. "Relational Integration, Part II: Relation Integration as Developmental and Intntercultural." *Journal of Psychology and Theology* 4, no. 3 (2015): 179-191.

Brown, Francis, Samuel Rolles Driver, and Charles Augustus Briggs. *Enhanced Brown-Driver-Briggs Hebrew and English Lexicon.* Oxford: Clarendon Press, 1977.

Bryant, Christopher. *Jung and the Christian Way.* San Francisco: Harper & Row, Publishers, 1983.

Bulkley, Ed. *Why Christians Can't Trust Psychology.* Eugene, OR: Harvest House Publishers, 1993.

Burkett, Larry. *Business by the Book: Biblical Principles for the Workplace.* Nashville, TN: Thomas Nelson, 1998.

Carson, D. A. "On Abusing Matthew 18." *Themelios*, 36, no. 1 (2011): 1-3.

Chrysostom, John. "Commentary of St. John Chrysostom, Archbishop of Constantinople, on the Epistle of St. Paul the Apostle to the Galatians." In *Saint Chrysostom: Homilies on Galatians, Ephesians, Philippians, Colossians, Thessalonians, Timothy, Titus, and Philemon. Vol. 13. A Select Library of the Nicene and Post-Nicene Fathers of the Christian Church, First Series.* Edited by Philip Schaff. New York: Christian Literature Company, 1889.

Clement of Alexandria, "The Instructor." In *Fathers of the Second Century: Hermas, Tatian, Athenagoras, Theophilus, and Clement of Alexandria (Entire)*. Vol. 2. *The Ante-Nicene Fathers*. Edited by Alexander Roberts, James Donaldson, and A. Cleveland Coxe. Buffalo, NY: Christian Literature Company, 1885.

Cloud, Henry and John Townsend. *Boundaries: When to Say Yes, How to Say No, How to Take Control of Your Life*. Grand Rapids, MI: Zondervan, 1992.

Dockery, David S., Trent C. Butler, et al. *Holman Bible Handbook*. Nashville, TN: Holman Bible Publishers, 1992.

Eldwell, Walter A. and Barry J. Beitzel. *Baker Encyclopedia of the Bible*. Grand Rapids, MI: Baker Book House, 1988.

Ellis, Larry D. *Forgiveness: Unleashing a Transformational Process*. Denver, CO: Adoration Publishing, 2010.

_____. *Radical Worship: What Sunday Morning Can Never Give You*. Denver, CO: Adoration Publishing Company, 2014.

Enroth, Ronald M. *Churches that Abuse*. Grand Rapids, MI: Zondervan Publishing House, 1993.

Erickson, Millard J. *Christian Theology*. Grand Rapids, MI: Baker Publishing Group, 1983.

Friedman, Edwin H. *A Failure of Nerve: Leadership in the Age of the Quick Fix*. New York, NY: Church Publishing, Inc., 2007.

Gaultiere, Bill. "Jesus Set Boundaries." http://www.soulshepherding.org/1998/07/jesus-set-boundaries/.

Gilbert, Roberta M. *Extraordinary Relationships: A New Way of Thinking about Human Interactions*. New York: John Wiley & Sons, Inc., 1992.

Grenz, Stanley J. *The Social God and the Relational Self.* Louisville: Westminster John Knox Press, 2001.

―――. *Theology for the Community of God.* Grand Rapids, MI: Wm. B. Eerdmans Publishing Co., 2000.

Jolley, Marc A. "Retribution." In *Eerdmans Dictionary of the Bible.* Edited by David Noel Freedman, Allen C. Myers, and Astrid B. Beck. Grand Rapids, MI: W.B. Eerdmans, 2000.

Kuepfer, Tim. "Matthew 18 Revisited." *Vision: A Journal for Church and Theology,* 8, no. 1.

Lynn, Anna. "Enmeshment and the Kingdom of God." *Thoughts by Annalynn.* May 4, 2013. Accessed May 16, 2016. https://thoughtsbyannalynn.wordpress.com/2013/07/04/enmeshment-and-the-kingdom-of-god/.

Majerus, Brian D. and Steven J Sandage. "Differentiation of Self and Christian Spiritual Maturity: Social Science and Theological Integration." *Journal of Psychology and Theology* 38, no. 1, (2010): 41-51.

McKnight, Scot. *The Blue Parakeet: Rethinking How You Read the Bible.* Grand Rapids, MI: Zondervan, 2008.

McWhirter, Jocelyn. "Nathan the Prophet." In *The Lexham Bible Dictionary.* Edited by John D. Barry et al. Bellingham, WA: Lexham Press, 2015.

Neville, Richard. "Differentiation in Genesis 1: An Exegetical Creation ex hihilo." *Journal of Biblical Literature,* 130, no. 2 (2011).

Pelikan, Jaroslav. *Whose Bible Is It?: A Short History of the Scriptures.* London: Penguin Group, 2004.

Powell, Mark Allan. "Canon." In *The HarperCollins Bible Dictionary* (Revised and Updated). Edited by Mark Allan Powell. New York: HarperCollins, 2011.

Richards, E. Randolph and Brandon J. O'Brien. *Misreading Scripture With Western Eyes*. Downers Grove, IL: InterVarsity Press, 2012.

Rogers, Ronnie W. *Undermining the Gospel: The Case and Guide for Church Discipline*. Bloomington, IL: WestBow Press, 2015.

Ross, Allen P. "Genesis." In *The Bible Knowledge Commentary: An Exposition of the Scriptures*. Vol. 1. Edited by J. F. Walvoord and R. B. Zuck. Wheaton, IL: Victor Books, 1985.

Sandage, Steven J. and Jeannine K. Brown. "Relational Integration, Part I: Differentiated Relationality between Psychology and Theology." *Journal of Psychology and Theology*, 43, no. 3 (2015): 165-178.

_____. "Relational Integration, Part II: Differentiated Relationality Between Psychology and Theology." *Journal of Psychology and Theology*, 43, no 3 (2015):179-191.

Schaeffer, Francis A. *The Complete Works of Francis A. Schaeffer: A Christian Worldview*, vol. 2. Westchester, IL: Crossway Books, 1982.

Soanes, Catherine and Angus Stevenson, eds. *Concise Oxford English Dictionary*. Oxford: Oxford University Press, 2004.

Stauffer, Edith R. *Unconditional Love and Forgiveness*. Diamond Springs, CA: Triangle Publishers, 1987.

VanKatwyk, Peter L. "Healing Through Differentiation: A Pastoral Care and Counseling Perspective." *The Journal of Pastoral Care*, 51, no. 3 (Fall 1997): 283-292.

VanVonderen, Jeff and Dale and Juanita Ryan. *Soul Repair: Rebuilding Your Spiritual Life*. Downers Grove, IL: Intervarsity Press, 2008.

Wohlfarth, Hannsdieter. *Johann Sebastian Bach*. Philadelphia, PA: Fortress Press, 1985.

Woods, Walter J. "Reconciliation and Priesthood," in *The Complete Library of Christian Worship*. Vol. 1, *The Biblical Foundations of Christian Worship,* edited by Robert E. Webber, 347-348. Nashville, TN: Star Song Pub. Group, 1993.

Index of Topics

Abednego 72-73
Adam and Eve 2, 80
aggressiveness xv, xvii
anger 9, 22, 43, 67, 69, 101
Anna Lynn 31, 110
assertiveness xv, xvii, 19, 112
authority 13, 29, 46, 73, 79-106, 110, 116, 128, 131, 133
authority over children 100-101
authority over people 87-100
Bach, J. S. 132-133
balloons 17-18
Bathsheba 66
Beare, Jerry 101
biology 49
Borchert, Gerald 90-91, 94-95
boundaries xi, xv, xvii, 1, 4, 13, 17-19, 21-22, 26, 34-36, 38, 47-48, 59-77, 81, 91, 100-101, 107-108, 111-112, 114-115, 117, 119
boundaries of Jesus 59-62
Brauch, Manfred T. 31
Burkett, Larry 28
chaos 44
Chrysostom, John 92-94
conflicting truths 79-81
control xix, 12, 1, 14, 18-19, 22-23, 50, 75-76, 88, 91, 100-101, 127
counseling 1, 4, 11, 113, 117, 121-135
counseling, biblical 123-128
counseling, holistic 128-134
counseling, secular 122-123
counterfeit xi, 16, 26, 30, 32,-33, 39, 110, 135

counterfeit unity 26, 29-33
Daniel 71-72
Dave 10-13
David (king) 66-69, 75
dependence 20, 63
detachment 35, 37, *also see disconnection*
die to self 108-109
differentiation xi, xvii, 4, 19, 28, 34, 38-39, 41, 44-51, 53, 62, 65-66, 75, 109, 114, 116-117
disconnection xi, 4, 16, 27, 35-39, 48-50, 62, 75-76, 111-114, 116-117
diversity 41, 44, 46, 51, 55-56, 81
DNA 49
Dockery, David 41-42
dominion 2, 45-46, 81
Donaldson, Jerry xv-xvi
Dunn, Jan 107-108
dysfunction 1, 2, 4, 7, 13, 16, 20-21, 23, 25-26, 29, 38, 56, 65, 76-77, 107, 109, 117, 122, 124, 135
emotions xi, xvii, 1, 3, 7, 16-23, 25, 27, 33, 37, 39, 42-43, 47-48, 60, 65, 76-77, 88, 95, 107-109, 125
emotions of God 42-43
endowment 54
enmeshment xi, xv, 4, 16-17, 19-30, 33-36, 47, 49-50, 62, 68, 70-71, 81, 83, 102-103, 107-112, 115-117, 135
enmeshment with God 4, 27-29, 33, 47, 102-103
ex nihilo 108
ezer 31
fall (the fall) 2

144 | Great Connections

false identity *xi, 20*
fear *xvi, 22, 33, 35, 68, 70, 72, 74, 77, 98*
feelings *3, 15, 17, 22-24, 36, 48, 75, 92, 113, 116-118*
forbearance *93-95*
fused *xi, 21, 39, 55, 108*
Gaultiere, Bill *59*
Gilbert, Roberta *38, 48-49, 114-115*
hearing God *83-87*
helper *31*
Holy Spirit *3, 26, 43, 47, 55, 82, 86, 99, 103*
image of God (imago dei) *45-46, 53, 56-57, 83, 111, 117, 127, 133*
immanent *43*
individuation *xi, xv, 4, 23, 50, 114-115*
intimacy *xi, 1, 5, 21, 26, 36, 47, 98, 110*
James *42, 53*
Job *70-71*
Jonathan *7-10*
liberation *2, 50, 107-119*
limitation *18*
Luther, Martin *74, 133*
Malachi *42*
manipulation *83*
Meshach *69, 72-73*
mirror *54, 91*
Moses *68-70, 75*
Nathan *66-69*
natural revelation *128*
Nouwen, Henri *v*
ownership *3, 13, 17, 48, 50-51, 55, 135*
Paul *3, 26, 32, 47, 84, 86, 89-91, 93-99, 101, 106, 109, 112, 124-127, 129, 132-133*
prodigal son *62-66*

purpose for being *54*
Rebecka *14-16*
rebuke *61, 70, 92, 94, 100*
reconciliation *2, 16, 37, 81-82, 98-98, 100,113-114*
respect *4, 13, 15, 17, 19, 22-23, 36, 47, 55, 65, 68, 75, 83, 87, 101, 105, 111, 114-117*
responsibility *xix, 1-3, 19, 49-51, 57, 74, 81, 88-89, 95, 99, 101, 110, 114*
retaliation *83, 98, 112*
retribution *32*
Richard *14-16*
Ross, Allen *44*
Schaeffer, Francis A, *45, 128-130*
Scripture *2, 4, 28-29, 31, 41-44, 46, 51, 53, 55, 59, 66, 69-70, 74-77, 82-86, 89, 96, 99-100, 103, 106, 121-131, 133-135*
self–authentic *xi, 108-109*
Shadrack *72-73*
social science *1, 128-129, 131*
Stauffer, Edith *113*
stem cells *49*
submission *31, 90, 95-96*
transcendent *43*
Trinity *51, 55-56*
uniformity *29-30, 41, 43-44, 46*
unity *26, 29-30, 33, 43-44, 47, 53, 55-57, 82*
Uriah *66-69, 76*
Wilberforce, William *132-133*
wise counsel *4, 84, 134*

Scripture Index

Genesis
1:2, *44*
1:3-5, *44*
1:6-7, *44*
1:9, *45*
1:11-12, *45*
1:20-21, *45*
1:24, *45*
1:26, *45*
1:27, *46*
1:28, *2*
2, *81*
2:18, *31*
3, *2, 81*
4, *32*
6-9, *32*
6:6, *43*

Exodus
3:14, *42*
18:4, *31*
20, *68*
22:34, *43*
32:10-20, *69*
33:19, *43*

Deuteronomy
5:26, *42*
6:14-15, *43*
7:7-8, *43*
13:1, *43*
25:4, *12, 5*
33:7, *31*
33:26, *31*
33:29, *31*

Judges
2:18, *43*

2 Samuel
7, *67*
11-12, *66*

11:27, *66*
12:7-11, *67*
12:12, *68*

Ezra
5:13, *43*

Job
1:20-21, *71*
2:9, *71*

Psalms
19:1-6, *128*
33:20, *31*
37:4, *86-87*
46:1, *31*
46:10a, *83*
51:10, *81*
103:3, *43*
103:13, *43*
115:9-11, *31*
116:5, *43*
119:10, *83*
119:105, *83, 96*
135:5-9, *42*
145:8, *43*

Proverbs
11:14, *28*
15:4, *84, 106*
15:22, *28*
27:17, *135*

Isaiah
43:4, *43*
62:4-5, *43*

Jeremiah
7:20, *43*
17:9, *87*
29:11-13, *85*
31:13, *43*

31:33, *81*
32:41, *43*

Ezekiel
36:25-28, *81*

Daniel
1, *72*
1:8, *72*
3, *73*
3:16-18, *73*
6, *72*

Hosea
11:1, *43*

Malachi
3:6, *42*

Matthew
5-7, *3, 32*
5:23-24, *100*
5:37, *61*
6:6, *61*
9:9-13, *98*
9:36, *43*
11:19, *98*
12:46-50, *60*
13:53-58, *61*
14:14, *43*
15:32, *43*
16:23, *61*
18, *97*
18:15-17, *97*
19:21-22, *134*
20:34, *43*
21:12-13, *43*
22:15-22, *61*
26:38, *60*
28:18-20, *82*

Mark
3:34 *108*
8:2, *43*
10:21, *43*
11:15-17, *43*

Luke
4:16-18, *60*
5:16, *60*
10:7, *125*
10:25-37, *134*
15, *62*
15:11, *63*
15:22-24, *64*
15:29-30, *64*
15:32, *43*
16:13, *61*
19:1-10, *98*
19:45-46, *43*
24:46-47, *43*

John
2:13-17, *22*
2:14-17, *43*
3:1-10, *32*
3:1-26, *134*
3:16, *43*
4:24, *43, 54*
5:17, *42*
6:51, *43*
10:11, *43*
10:18, *110*
10:27, *83*
11:35, *43*
11:50-52, *43*
13:1, *43*
13:1-10, *32*
13:34-35, *31*
13:36, *56*
14:15-17, *86*
17:20-24, *56*
17:28, *43*

Acts
3:4, *9, 134*
6:5, *43*
10:16, *134*

17:1-2, *134*
20:35, *59*

Romans
1:20, *129*
3:9, *81*
3:23, *109*
5:1-11, *82*
5:12, *81*
8, *86*
8:29, *54*
11:33, *42*
12:2, *84*
12:10, *109*
12:17-21, *112*
14:12, *91*

1 Corinthians
5, *99*
6:19, *43*
10:31, *132*
14:20, *96*

2 Corinthians
5:18-19, *82*
6:16, *43*

Galatians
5:16-24, *3*
6, *90, 92*
6:1, *90*
6:1-5, *89*
6:2, *106*

Ephesians
1:11, *42*
3:11, *42*
4:12, *47*
4:29, *106*
6:4, *101*

Philippians
2:3-8, *32*

Colossians
1:9-10, *96*
1:19-22, *82*

1 Thessalonians
4:9-10, *109*
5:11, *106*

1 Timothy
3:9-10, *126*
3:14-16, *126*
3:17, *126*
5:18, *125*

2 Timothy
3:16-17, *124*

Hebrews
10:24-25, *106*
12:10, *101*
12:16-17, *95*
13:16-18, *95*
13:17, *90*

James
1:17, *42*
3:9, *54*

1 Peter
1:22-24, *109*
2:21-24, *43*
2:23, *113*
4:8, *109*

2 Peter
1:3-4, *126*
1:5-12, *127, 134*
3:15-16, *125*

1 John
3:11, *109*
3:23, *109*
4:7, *109*
4:8, *10, 19, 43*
4:8b, *108*
4:11-12, *109*
4:16a, *108*

2 John
5:5, *109*

Other Books Written by the Author

In *Forgiveness: Unleashing a Transformational Process* Larry D. Ellis addresses one of the most challenging topics, the receiving and giving of forgiveness. He addresses the historic Christian perspective of forgiveness being the sole responsibility of the one who has been hurt or offended. Ellis puts forth an extensive development from ancient documents, pivotal biblical passages, especially Jesus' Sermon on the Mount, and a number of traumatizing realities of the current time. His chapter on the Fictional Myths of Forgiveness is particularly insightful, exposing a number of cultural perspectives that presents a counterfeit imitation of forgiveness, which will never lead to full reconciliation between persons in great conflict.

www.theforgivenessbook.com

In *Secrets for a Successful Small Business: What the University Will Not Teach You*, the author draws from over forty years of seasoned experience as an entrepreneur. He has founded and operated small businesses in a wide range of industries. This book presents a breadth of important, but hard-to-find topics, for small business owners. Chapters include selection of business structure, selecting, hiring and firing of employees, web site development, advertising, marketing, telecommunications needs, business insurance, travel, children in the workplace, religious expression on the job, trade show participation, travel, taxes, profitability and cash flow analysis, and dozens of other important topics for the small business owner.

www.thesmallbusinessbook.com

In *Radical Worship: What Sunday Morning Can Never Give You,* the reader will learn that the foundation of all our lives is the worship of God. The author reclaims the biblical meaning of worship, stepping away from the popular meanings used today. He discusses the direct relationship between submitting to God and the re-creation of who we are in Christ. He focuses on the words that are translated worship in both the Old Testament and the New Testament. Additionally, the significance of worship is examined through Jesus' responses to the question, "What must I do to inherit eternal life?" The author critiques some of the narrowness of formulaic Christianity and unfolds some of the many expressions of worship that Jesus explicitly affirms.

www.theradicalworshipbook.com

www.ingramcontent.com/pod-product-compliance
Lightning Source LLC
LaVergne TN
LVHW051601070426
835507LV00021B/2706